HELP
for the Helper

The Psychophysiology of Compassion Fatigue and Vicarious Trauma

HELP
for the **Hel/per**

The Psychophysiology of Compassion Fatigue and Vicarious Trauma

BABETTE ROTHSCHILD

with

MARJORIE L. RAND

W.W. Norton & Company
New York • London

The author welcomes correspondence from readers. She may be reached at:
Babette Rothschild
P.O. Box 241778
Los Angeles, California 90024
Telephone: 310 281 9646
E-mail: babette@trauma.cc
Web site: www.trauma.cc

For information about permission
to reproduce selections from this book, write to
Permissions, W. W. Norton & Company, Inc.,
500 Fifth Avenue, New York, NY 10110

Production Manager: Leeann Graham
Manufacturing by R.R. Donnelley-Harrisonburg

Library of Congress Cataloging-in-Publication Data

Rothschild, Babette.
  Help for the helper : the psychophysiology of compassion fatigue and vicarious
trauma / Babette Rothschild, with Marjorie L. Rand
       p.   ; cm.
"A Norton professional book."
Includes bibliographical references and index.
ISBN 0-393-70422-X
1. Post-traumatic stress disorder—Treatment. 2. Psychotherapists—Job stress.
3. Emergency medical personnel—Job stress. 4. Counselors—Job stress. I. Rand,
Marjorie L., 1944- II. Title.

RC552.P67R6856 2006
616.85'21—dc22   2005054037

W. W. Norton & Company, Inc., 500 Fifth Avenue, New York, N.Y. 10110
www.wwnorton.com

W. W. Norton & Company, Ltd., Castle House, 75/76 Wells St., London W1T 3QT

5 7 9 0 8 6

This book is dedicated to all of the helpers

Contents

Preface
Using Common Sense

In the introduction to *The Body Remembers Casebook* (2003a), I discussed the importance of applying common sense to work with trauma. Generally, I find both the skill and trend sorely missing in the practice of psychotherapy, so I speak about common sense regularly in lectures and training programs. It continues to amaze me that many, many people approach me during breaks to say how "important" or "refreshing" it is to "finally" hear someone talk about using common sense. When I take an informal poll of how many in my audience were taught or encouraged to use their own innate common sense during their education or professional training, somewhere between 10% and 33% raise their hands. I have never seen as much as half the audience with their hands up. Though I am proud to contribute to filling this neglected gap, I am appalled that it is necessary. Every training program in psychotherapy (university, organization, agency, or institution alike) should be teaching, promoting, and supporting the use of common sense *alongside* the other theory and tools that are being taught. The success of both the psychotherapy of clients and the self-care of psychotherapists is greatly enhanced by the liberal application of common sense. With regard to the topic of this book, *Help for the Helper*, applying common sense could save heaps of professional pain and suffering. Moreover, it could also probably save agencies and HMOs plenty of actual dollars.

Temple Grandin (2005), author of *Thinking in Pictures* and *Animals in Translation,* is the well-known animal behaviorist who also is afflicted with high-functioning autisim. Her brilliance in designing handling systems for livestock (which she has done over much of the United States and Canada) is not only rooted in her talent for visualization, but is also largely the product of common sense. Her cornerstone is a simple assumption: If animals are scared, then something is scaring them. For her it is that simple. As a result, she counsels that no matter how much you use an electric prod, the animals will still be afraid to cooperate and will balk at what you want them to do. The more you prod, the more afraid they will be. Grandin demonstrates time and again that simply identifying and changing or removing the source of their fear—the "trigger," as we would say—(often something as simple as covering a reflective piece of metal) removes the need for electric prods. The animals just become calmly cooperative.

The same principle applies to us. If we are suffering under the weight of our work or from interactions with particular clients, then identifying and changing the triggering circumstances should give us much-needed relief. Of course, sometimes making these changes is easier said than done. But the principle is the same: Use your common sense to identify your work stressors and develop strategies to intervene. Here is one example.

> *During a recent consultation, a fairly experienced therapist complained of severe stress due to feelings of failure and guilt. He had been struggling with one of his clients and felt unable to help. Probing, I discovered that he actually did not have the knowledge base necessary to work with that type of client. From the perspective of common sense, I saw two basic options: (1) refer the client to someone who does have the skills and knowledge that are needed, or (2) hire a supervisor or consultant who could coach him through or teach him what is needed along the*

*way. Either choice would go a long way to assuaging both
guilt and failure feelings, and the client would actually be
helped. I further advised that the therapist make peace
with reality: No single therapist can—or should—treat
all clients. That is also common sense.*

Amid the theory and exercises in this book, you will also
find (what I hope are) generous helpings of common sense.
I expect—and welcome—that some readers will finish this
book and say, "Yes, how simple!" in reaction to portions of
the theory and skills presented. Much of it really is simple.
Becoming adept at self-care does not require long training
programs (though I do love to give workshops on these topics). Mostly, you just need to use your common sense.

HELP
for the **Helper**
The Psychophysiology of Compassion Fatigue and Vicarious Trauma

Introduction

*Toward the end of the Haunted Mansion ride at Disney-
land, the black coach I'm riding in turns to face a mirror. I
can clearly see the reflections of myself and the friends I'm
riding with. There is also the faded reflection of one or
more ghosts who appear to be riding along with us in our
laps. They are smiling and carrying suitcases, intent on
hitching a ride home with us. Of course, at the end of the
ride, there are not really any ghosts hanging on to us nor
are they in the car when we get home.*

With our clients, however, that is not always the
case. Sometimes it seems that some of them are more successful than the Haunted Mansion ghosts: In essence, they
hitch a ride home with us—or, more accurately, inside of us.
Often we are not aware that we have brought home an un-
welcome visitor unless we notice that we are agitated rather
than relaxed, have trouble sleeping, or pick a useless fight
with our partner and make the connection.

When this happens once in a great while, the consequences
are usually minimal. But for practitioners who consistently
bring their clients home—consciously or unconsciously—
the impact over time can be severe. This book's mission is to
prevent just that, and to promote the stance that we need not
bring our clients home with us to qualify as compassionate or
competent practitioners. In fact, the opposite may actually
be the case: *The better we take care of ourselves and maintain a professional separation from our clients, the more
we will be in a position to be truly empathetic, compassionate, and useful to them.*

It is my hope that this book will radically change the ways in which psychotherapists conceptualize, as well as act on, the risks of their profession, including compassion fatigue and vicarious traumatization. Additionally, I hope to influence current thinking about ways in which therapists are affected by their clients. Along the way, I will discuss the science of these phenomena and offer practical strategies that will aid the therapist in taking charge of these potential hazards rather than feeling at their mercy.

Of course, psychotherapists are not the only helping professionals who are affected by these and other phenomena discussed in this volume. However, since therapists comprise the vast majority of potential readers, vocabulary and examples are aimed at them. However, as with my first book, *The Body Remembers: The Psychophysiology of Trauma and Trauma Treatment* (Rothschild, 2000), I expect that a good number of readers will be members of the other helping professions (doctors, nurses, emergency workers, massage and other body therapists, administrators, etc.) and others will be laypersons. Please feel free to translate the examples and exercises into your own language and realm of professional or personal experience. You are welcome to try out and share any of the exercises in this book with your own supervisees, colleagues, and students. In addition, if you have any questions or if you have particularly positive or negative results from using the skill-building sections, please let me know (my contact information is on the copyright page following the title page—e-mail is easiest).

OVERVIEW

Negative consequences of therapeutic work are often unconscious. All too many therapists career toward burnout without noticing it. Therefore, the major goal of this book is to equip practitioners with tools that will increase their awareness and reduce their vulnerability to the factors that could lead to compassion fatigue, vicarious trauma, and burnout. Some of the case examples involve therapists who work with traumatized individuals, because the impact of client traumas poses an additional risk to the therapist. However, this book is written for all psychotherapists—also those not working with traumatized clients. Anyone of us can be adversely affected by our work.

Therapist self-care requires the proper functioning of at least three neuropsychological systems. All three are necessary for the therapist to be fully in control of her own well-being even in the most distressing of situations.* The first involves the brain mechanisms that operate in interpersonal empathy. The second depends on balance in the autonomic nervous system (ANS) and arousal regulation. The third requires clear thinking that relies, in part, on the balanced functioning of all brain structures. In short, for a therapist to minimize risks to her emotional and physical well-being, she needs to be able to find ways to balance her empathetic engagement, regulate her ANS arousal, and maintain her ability to think clearly.

Theories already exist about the cognitive mechanisms and psychological impact of therapeutic risks. However, for the most part, the neuropsychological and somatic aspects have yet to be studied in depth. This volume introduces solid research from neurobiological, experimental, social, and folk psychology that will explain the origins of the risks therapists encounter in their work with clients. Scientific findings then form the foundation for the design and support of new skills therapists can use to improve their own situations.

Though neuroscience is daunting for some, I would urge the reader to take the time to understand it. The risks to therapist well-being that are addressed here are all intimately linked to the body and brain. Knowing how you are affected by your clients will enhance your control over those effects.

---

* I have alternated the use of the pronouns *he* and *she* throughout the text and hope to have been equitable.

Of course, not all of the many interventions and skill-building exercises offered in each chapter will suit everyone. Understanding your own psychophysiology will put you in a good position to choose skills and tailor additional interventions to your own individual needs. Moreover, comprehending these processes will give you the potential to create and develop skills that are particularly suited to you.

On Assessment

For those readers who prefer to use tests to determine if they are suffering from compassion fatigue, vicarious trauma, or burnout, several scales and instruments are provided in Appendix 1 at the end of the book. However, all such tools need to be used with large helpings of common sense. Most of them are designed for use in large research studies and for insurance purposes; they are not typically suited to individual use.

Your best tool for evaluating your own personal situation will be self-awareness, body awareness, and your own common sense. Throughout this volume in theory and skill sections and case examples, various difficulties that can arise in psychotherapeutic work are described alongside suggestions for intervention. As a whole, this book will provide you with a basis for identifying when you might be having difficulty or moving in that direction. However, there is no way to cover everything. Remember, when in doubt, fall back on your common sense and knowledge about yourself.

A Word About Burnout

Burnout is a term commonly used in many professions, not just the helping professions, to describe the consequences of varying forms of job stress. In the vernacular, it can mean anything from the need for an extra day off to becoming totally dysfunctional or decompensated. Many factors can lead to burnout, some of which are covered in this volume. Beyond the scope of these pages, however, are stressors that stem from workplace structural or administrative issues, and from personal (nonprofessional) relationships and circumstances.

Why All Those Pages on Psychology?

Knowledge is power. The more you understand how you are affected by your clients, the more you will have the choice to maximize those effects when beneficial, and minimize them when they pose increased risks to your—or your client's—well-being.

Thankfully, in recent years, neuroscience and other branches of scientific study have turned their attention to interpersonal relationships. That literature has produced a wealth of information that can be used and adapted in the therapeutic setting.

Many of my therapist colleagues shy away from scientific theory because they are bewildered by it or have no clue how to apply it. They complain to me that seminars only teach theory, which is easy to forget in a few weeks. Practical application and practice are often missing from professional training experiences. For that reason, this book includes many case examples as well as exercises in an effort to bridge the gap between theory and application.

ORGANIZATION

Throughout the book, several concepts and techniques are illustrated with transcripts that are composites of professional consultation sessions. Most of those sessions focus on the psychological and somatic experience of the practitioner and ways to mediate risk factors. Such body-oriented professional guidance will not be new to many body psychotherapists, though some specific interventions may be. In general, it is my hope that supervisors and consultants in mainstream and alternative realms of psychology will be encouraged to pay more attention to what is happening in themselves and in the bodies of the therapists they are assisting.

Chapter 1 introduces the basic concepts that are explored throughout the book. Chapters 2 through 4 each discuss theory and skill building in their respective topics. The theoretical sections include discussion of the most relevant research, past and present. Each skill-building section is linked to the theory of that chapter, so that each management strategy fits within the context of the science being discussed. This maximizes the likelihood that individuals will be equipped to further develop their own strategies and build skills that are not already in their repertoire. Case examples illustrate common therapist dilemmas. Exercises follow to enable the learning of new skills and strategies for improved coping. Chapter 5 ties together both the theory and skills discussed throughout the book. Two appendices appear at the end. One offers scales and inventories for assessing levels of professional distress. The other reviews three ongoing research projects on topics related to this book.

It is suggested that the reader approach each skill-building section as an *experiment*. Try the skill out before you commit yourself to adding it to your repertoire. The skills proposed here are intended to increase your options for self-care, to add more choices to your toolbox, *not* to decrease them. Please *do not* abandon any tools you already find useful.

This book is about therapist self-care, including reducing vulnerability with clients and paying attention to optimal separation and boundaries. It is important, however, to keep in mind that being open and vulnerable with clients can also be of use—sometimes just the right thing. It is not my aim to radically change your way of working, but merely to help you recognize your areas of vulnerability and give you more choices in managing them.

There is a wealth of literature on most of the topics discussed among these pages, some of it overlapping. I have reviewed much of it, but have surely missed some. Where possible, I have endeavored to identify the originators of terms and concepts and to cite ideas accurately. If, however, I have erred in giving appropriate credit to any publication or individual, I would appreciate being notified of my oversight. On the page following the title page you will find author and publisher contact information.

DISCLAIMER

Disclaimers appear in the introductions to my previous two books (Rothschild, 2000, 2003). I carry on that tradition here with another, pertinent to this subject matter.

The pages of this volume are filled with both historical—tried-and-true—and cutting-edge theories. Please keep in mind that a theory is just that; it is not fact. In science, facts are few. They are even scarcer in the branch of science called psychology. Among these pages, I express my own considered opinions, based on the considered opinions of others. Readers are encouraged to formulate their own opinions and to not regard mine as the last word.

No one expresses this sentiment better than Antonio Damasio: "I am skeptical of science's presumption of objectivity and definitiveness. I have a difficult time seeing scientific results, especially in neurobiology, as anything but provisional approximations, to be enjoyed for a while and discarded as soon as better accounts become available" (1994, p. xviii). What follows are the best approximations (mine and others') available at the time the final manuscript went to press.

Chapter 1

Psychotherapists at Risk

We are born with the capacity . . . to experience what others experience and participate in their experience by virtue of the way we are grabbed by their nervous system. One of the real questions is not, "How in the world does this happen?" We're beginning to have a really good idea. The real question is "How do we stop it from happening so that we are not the prisoner of someone else's nervous system all the time." There have got to be a lot of brakes in the system, and probably that will be a very interesting area of research which has not been addressed so far.

—*Daniel N. Stern* (2002)

All emotions are contagious—both the ones that are pleasant and the ones that are unpleasant. The entertainment industry capitalizes on this feature of emotion, tugging at our feelings with strong affects portrayed by actors, and infecting us with the raw emotions of reality programs. The popularity of makeover shows is a great example. Typically, at the end of these shows an individual or family is presented with something near and dear that has been incredibly transformed (bodies, cars, homes, etc.). The joy and excitement that is always expressed by the recipients is so contagious that it is impossible not to feel happy with them as well as for them. These shows take advantage of emotional contagion to manipulate our feelings. As helping professionals, our emotions are also vulnerable to provocation through infection with our clients' feelings. Sometimes this is an advantage, helping us to feel inside their worlds. At other times, it is not advantageous to be infected by a client's state.

THERAPIST ASSETS AND DEFICITS

The capacity that Stern alludes to in the quote above is *empathy*. As psychotherapists, empathy is our major, greatest, and most reliable tool. Often it is our capacity for empathy that brings us to the helping professions in the first place. As Stern said, we have "the capacity to experience what others experience." Empathy allows us to relate to those in our care, to have a sense of what they are feeling. It also helps us put their experiences into perspective, understanding how they are being affected by the incidents that we are trying to mediate. When we have an insight, an accurate hunch, or seem to read the client's mind, that may also be a result of empathy. Without it, we could not be the effective therapists that we are. Empathy is an integral, necessary tool of our work.

That is one of the benefits of empathy. At the same time, it has detriments. If empathy is such a central and beneficial tool of psychotherapy, why do so many of our dedicated and experienced colleagues reel from working with distressed clients? Is it possible that empathy is actually a double-edged sword, wielding both help and harm? Does the same tool that facilitates our understanding of our clients also threaten our well-being at times? The short answer is yes. It is my hypothesis that many therapists suffer in their work as a result of *un-*

conscious empathy—that is, empathy processes that are outside of the therapist's awareness and therefore also outside of his control. Many of the common therapist pitfalls have roots in, or at least a relationship to, unconscious empathy gone awry, including the phenomena defined later in this chapter: unmanageable countertransference, projective identification, compassion fatigue, vicarious traumatization, and burnout.

Why are therapists suffering as a result of their jobs? Certainly, general problems of the workplace can contribute to burnout. When hours, client loads, compensation, colleague and administrative conflicts, bullying, and so on are inadequately managed, any employee on any job can suffer. However, those types of problems are beyond the scope of this book. Here the focus must be on the consequences of the interaction between the therapist and the client. When and why can the act of helping actually hurt the therapist? Could it be that some psychotherapists are just ill-suited for their line of work? Or is it more likely, as Stern implied, that a therapist can become "the prisoner of someone else's nervous system"—the nervous system of a client?

Some of the clues to answering these questions are to be found in the branch of psychotherapy that specializes in treatment of traumatized individuals. Since the diagnosis of post-traumatic stress disorder (PTSD) entered the American Psychiatric Association's *Diagnostic and Statistical Manual of Mental Disorders (DSM)* in 1980, work with traumatized individuals and groups has become popular. Over the ensuing years, it has also become commonplace for psychotherapists, as well as their consultants and supervisors, to observe negative consequences from working with traumatized clients. The consequences extend beyond the impact on the psychotherapists who suffer. Their workplaces can lose out from lost work hours due to sick days and personal leave, worker's compensation claims, and the expense of early retirement. Also, of course, relationships with family and friends can be hurt when clients are allowed to intrude into a therapist's personal life.

It is not new for therapists to suffer negative consequences from working with traumatized individuals. However, it is new for the professional community to pay attention to it in an organized manner. The first books to recognize such risks were published in the mid-1990s and focused on those working with trauma: Wilson and Lindy's (1994) *Countertransference in the Treatment of PTSD*, Figley's (1995) *Compassion Fatigue*, Stamm's (1995) *Secondary Traumatic Stress*, and Pearlman and Saakvitne's (1995) *Trauma and the Therapist*. Each of these books has contributed to the field with relevant theories. They all include recommendations for therapists to pay more attention to their personal and professional needs, including obtaining regular consultation. However, none of them have looked at what is going on *inside* the therapist who succumbs to the impact of his client's trauma—what is happening in his brain and body. And none has looked beyond behavioral interventions. In this volume, readers will learn how client distress affects the therapist's brain and body and will receive training in somatic and cognitive skills to both increase awareness and mediate the effects.

IDENTIFYING TERMINOLOGY

Four terms have become popular (as reflected in the book titles above) to describe the negative risks therapists face: *compassion fatigue, vicarious traumatization, secondary traumatization*, and *burnout*. (citation for these terms are detailed below). From a search on the PsycINFO database, it appears that burnout is the oldest of these concepts, first mentioned in relationship to mental health workers in (Pines & Maslach, 1978). The term *vicarious traumatization* first appeared in 1985 in a therapist journal article on the vulnerability of children to the trauma of others (Terr, 1985). It then entered the therapist vocabulary as a descriptor of negative effects on psychotherapists with the publication of McCann and Pearlman's (1990) "Vicarious Traumatization: A

Framework for Understanding the Psychological Effects of Working With Victims." They applied the term *vicarious* in recognition that a therapist may vicariously experience aspects or effects of a client's trauma as if it had happened to herself.

Secondary traumatization seems to have first appeared in an article by Rosenheck and Nathan (1985). For many years, *secondary trauma* was used to describe the effect of traumatic contagion—how trauma symptoms can seemingly be caught just like a cold or the flu—between family members (Solomon, Waysman, & Levy, 1992; Waysman, Mikulincer, & Solomon, 1993; Benjamin & Benjamin, 1994). However, in 1995, *secondary trauma* took on a new meaning with the publication of Stamm's *Secondary Traumatic Stress*, an edited text on self-care for clinicians. She applied the term similarly to vicarious traumatization. That same year, Figley (1995) published another edited book on the same topic, coining a new term with his title, *Compassion Fatigue*. Figley's term, also used in the subtitle of this volume, has caught on as a readily understandable concept and catchphrase. Most psychotherapists, as well as those in other helping professions, recognize that their compassionate work can lead to exhaustion.

Also in 1995, Pearlman and Saakvitne published *Trauma and the Therapist*, expressing their own views on countertransference and vicarious traumatization in psychotherapists working with the special population of incest survivors. They were the first to spotlight what may be happening to a therapist during a psychotherapy session.

Since the publication of those three books, there has been some professional confusion about how, exactly, to use and distinguish the four terms: *burnout, secondary traumatization, vicarious traumatization,* and *compassion fatigue.* They are often used rather interchangeably in therapist literature and discussions. Some attempt was made by Pearlman and Saakvitne (1995) to circumscribe the concepts. A further stab at clarification follows.

These terms are used throughout this text with the meanings specified below. They are discussed in an effort to strike a compromise between conflicting definitions as they exist throughout the professional literature. These definitions are certainly still open to debate—as is vocabulary in any field. At the least, these should help make the content of this book clearer.

Compassion fatigue (Figley, 1995) is a general term applied to anyone who suffers as a result of serving in a helping capacity. Bonnita Wirth (see Chapter 3) gives a good description of unconscious compassion fatigue resulting from the stresses of psychotherapy practice.

Burnout is reserved for an extreme circumstance. It describes anyone whose health is suffering or whose outlook on life has turned negative because of the impact or overload of their work.

Primary traumatization is understood as the impact of a traumatic incident on the obvious victim of that incident. This includes survivors of all types of traumatic events, including those rescued from disaster sites, mental health clients, and medical patients injured by trauma such as a house fire. This category also includes any psychotherapists who have been directly affected by a traumatic incident through being injured or assaulted, losing a relative or close friend, and so on.

Secondary traumatization has two categories. The first involves family members and close associates who may suffer from their loved one's trauma as a result of the closeness of the relationship. An example would include the spouse of a rape victim.

The second category of secondary trauma involves therapists who are eyewitnesses to the incident they are meant to mediate. While not primary casualties of the event, they may become secondary victims by becoming overwhelmed by what they see and hear in person. Theirs is not a vicarious experience, but a direct experience of witnessing. People suffering from this type of secondary traumatization may also suffer from primary trauma as well, depending on the nature and degree of their exposure. This could include, for example, a therapist who witnessed the devastation of the September 11, 2001, attacks on the World Trade Center in New York City. If that therapist was also in danger himself—say he was one of those fleeing the collapsing buildings—then he could be considered a primary victim of trauma.

With regard to psychotherapists impacted by working with traumatized individuals in their workplaces, the term *vicarious traumatization* is used. Even when a therapist was not actually involved in the client's trauma, she can still vicariously experience it in her nervous system. The result is similar to feeling vicarious excitement while watching someone on a roller-coaster ride on television, or hearing a breathless detailed description of a horseback ride. The observers and listeners have not actually been exposed to the event, though they can really feel it. A pornographic movie has a similar mechanism and sometimes a more recognizable effect.

A note of clarification: When a psychotherapist suffers from, or is more vulnerable to, the effects of vicarious trauma due to a personal history of trauma, the historic trauma is primary; traumatic stress resulting from hearing descriptions of a client's trauma is vicarious.

Any of these phenomena can affect the psychotherapist. Compassion fatigue and burnout may have their roots in the psychotherapeutic relationship, but can also arise independently of the issues clients bring to therapy. Sometimes problems of workplace administration can be a contributing factor. Of course, any helping professional who neglects to satisfy her human needs for companionship, rest, reasonable working hours, free time, vacations, and so on, can eventually succumb to burnout. Vicarious traumatization, in particular, is a sign that a client's history is having an extreme effect on the therapist.

COUNTERTRANSFERENCE

Our difficulty here is to get one word [countertransference] *not* to
mean as many different things as there are people using it.
                                            —*Margaret Little* (1957)

For many, countertransference is a confusing and highly de-
batable concept. There are widely varying definitions of the
term, as well as wildly divergent strategies for managing it.

Before discussing countertransference, a brief review of the
concept of transference will help to put it into perspective. In
the early days of psychoanalysis, Sigmund Freud wanted the
mental state of his analysts to be like a blank screen. That
way, he believed, a patient could project or "transfer" his or
her feelings from past experiences onto the analyst. Freud
wanted this process to be uncomplicated by the analyst's own
feelings or biases. Through analysis of the patient's transference, analysts would be able to confront and come to terms
with fears and other feelings that often emanated from experiences in their own pasts.

As almost every psychotherapist now knows, it is impossible to keep one's mind blank and remain completely objective when facing a client's emotions. Even the best-trained
and most experienced psychotherapist is vulnerable to being
touched or stirred by his clients. Freud eventually recognized that the reactive feelings of analysts were inevitable
and coined a new term in 1910: "We have become aware of
the 'counter-transference' which arises in the Physician as a
result of the patient's influence on his unconscious feelings,
and we are most inclined to insist that he shall recognize this
counter-transference in himself and overcome it" (Freud,
1910/1953, pp. 141–142). In the same paper, he went on to
indicate that he expected the analyst to rise above countertransference reactions. He asserted that those who could not
do so should not become practitioners of psychoanalysis. In
a later paper, Freud went on to reinforce the idea that countertransference must be kept "in check" (Freud, 1915/1953,
p. 164).

Definitions of countertransference vary. Some believe it only involves the unconscious feelings stirred up in the therapist by the client. Others hold that countertransference encompasses the totality of the therapist's reaction to the client. Informally, many therapists think of transference as baggage from the client's past carried into the therapy room, and countertransference as the therapist's past baggage.

Not every therapist response to a client is a countertransference reaction. There are many other possible sources for a therapist's response to his clients. Three examples follow.

Some therapist reactions are appropriate responses for the circumstances, such as a therapist who becomes anxious or angry in response to an angry client who is acting in a threatening manner. Another class of reactions has roots in somatic empathy (discussed at length in Chapter 2), for example, getting a stomachache when a client has one. Still other reactions may be responses to client projections that have no echo or hook in the therapist's current or earlier life, as when a soft-spoken therapist becomes frustrated at a client's continued accusations that she is yelling.

Of course, today most practitioners disagree with Freud. While it can stir uncomfortable feelings, it is generally acknowledged that countertransference is sometimes desirable in the therapeutic relationship. At the least, it can help a therapist to enhance empathy or give him clues to understanding what is going on with the client.

In recent years, interpersonal analysts have questioned the traditional concept of transference (Gill, 1983; Gill & Hoffman, 1982; Stern, 1985a, 1992). They believe transference experiences are related to current therapeutic interactions and are not solely distortions or projections from the past. Gillard Hoffman (1982) says transference operates much like a Geiger counter, sensitizing an individual to ascribe meanings that might not be apparent or meaningful to anyone else.

Contemporary interpersonal psychoanalysts view the therapeutic relationship as an intersubjective one in which client

and analyst are influencing each other all the time (Stolorow
& Atwood,1992). Transference and countertransference are
seen as arising from the relationship jointly created by both,
an *interpersonal* rather than *intrapsychic* experience. In
other words, in this view, the client's transference creates the
analyst's countertransference; and conversely, the analyst's
countertransference creates the client's transference.

Marlene's situation illustrates one of the constructive uses
of countertransference:

> *Marlene knew that she felt deeply for her clients, espe-*
> *cially the ones struggling with depression. She realized*
> *that some of her feelings had roots in memories of her*
> *mother's depression. Countertransference helped her to*
> *gain a deep empathy with her depressed clients. Over*
> *many years, she became more successful with those clients*
> *than some of her colleagues who did not have a depressed*
> *parent.*

For the purposes of this book, the simplest definition is the
most useful. From here on, the term *countertransference*
will refer to the practitioner's reactions to his client that have
roots in his own past. For example, if the therapist becomes
sad when his client expresses grief because of her own unresolved grief, that is countertransference. If he becomes sad
when a long-term client reports that he has cancer, that is not
countertransference.

Countertransference in the Therapeutic Relationship

The therapeutic relationship usually consists of two people:
The therapist and the client. However, at times it may seem
as if there are others in the room, ghosts from each person's
past. Thus the therapeutic relationship actually consists of
two people and two personal histories. Essentially, transference and countertransference exist in any relationship, not
just the therapeutic relationship: parent-child, teacher-student,

employee-employer, between friends, and in couples. Inter-personal and relational patterns and dynamics from the past that have been internalized by each person may inevitably arise and be reenacted within many relationships. Transfer-ence and countertransference elements in a relationship can be positive or negative, healthy or unhealthy, or a benefit or deficit to the relationship (Kohut, 1981). For example, if your blue eyes remind me of my mother, and that brings up a warm feeling in me, then I may be more sympathetic or com-passionate toward you. If I perceive your distant attitude as being like my father's, I may think you do not like me. If your academic prowess reminds me of my older brother, I may feel competitive and resentful toward you. These old patterns arise in the current relationship though they are actually re-flections from the past. Managing countertransference to the best advantage is facilitated by mindfulness (being aware), including body awareness.

Ellen, a child psychologist, worked in a neighborhood agency. She had lost her mother when she was 3 years old. Her father subsequently married a woman with two daughters. Ellen never felt that she was treated fairly by her stepmother. As a result, she was particularly anxious about her child clients who had stepparents. As much of her caseload involved children of divorce, her anxiety was persistent and gradually increased to uncontainable levels. During a much-needed leave of absence, she sought ther-apy for herself. She became aware that unresolved issues from her own childhood were infringing on her ability to effectively help her young clients. Becoming aware of the corollaries and how they affected her was adequate to en-able her return to work. However, sticking with her own therapy proved to be important. Once she resolved the is-sues that were provoked by her clients, she was better able to help them without suffering along with them.

Countertransference can be identified from several sources. It is usually identified from thoughts and emotions; however, body sensations, mental images, and behaviors can also be important indicators.

Body sensations, including temperature changes, shifts in areas of tension and relaxation, skin sensations, and so on can be part of a countertransference response. If you have ever felt your skin crawl or become tense in your shoulders while with a client, you have likely experienced a somatic aspect of countertransference. Having pictures in your mind's eye or dialogue or songs in your mind's ear might also be part of such a response. Finally, noticing changes in your breathing or heart rate, or finding yourself moving or behaving in an unexpected way may be the result of countertransference (though some might call the latter projective identification, which is the topic of the next section).

Bobbe was usually a very calm and patient therapist. Every once in a while, though, she would find herself re-acting harshly to a client, particularly those who were judgmental of others. With some help from her supervisor, she realized that these episodes began with a growing ten-sion in her chest that restricted her breathing. She then would become very impatient and sometimes lash out. Bobbe's supervisor helped her to identify that the somatic and emotional scenario followed a course that was famil-iar. During her high school years, she endured many lec-tures from her judgmental older brother. The supervisor suggested Bobbe work on this memory in psychotherapy, which helped her to separate her judgmental clients from the judgments of her brother. As a result, Bobbe gained im-proved functioning with her clients and, as a bonus, with her now adult brother.

Countertransference Exercise

Here is a quick exercise that will give you more clarity about some aspects of countertransference. Choose one of your clients to focus on during this exercise. Feel free to write down your responses. First, imagine that client and notice the following:

- *Sensations you feel in your body* (hot, cold, achy, prickles, etc.)
- *Visual or auditory images that arise in your mind* (pictures, colors, sounds, songs, etc.)
- *Movement or muscular impulses in your body* (head turning, sitting back, legs tensing, clenched fists, etc.)
- *What you feel* (angry, irritated, sad, happy, scared, turned on, disgusted, etc.)
- *Any thoughts that occur to you*

Next, take a few minutes to consider which of your responses could be mirrors of your client's experience (sensations, images, behaviors, feelings, thoughts)? Which are more likely reflections from your own past?

There is nothing right or wrong about your answers in this (or any) exercise. Each point is significant: How you feel about your client and what that client elicits in you. Feel free to try this exercise with other clients. It might be interesting to see how your experiences differ from client to client.

PROJECTIVE IDENTIFICATION

Projective identification is a major psychoanalytic theory. It attempts to account for how and why analysts sometimes find themselves having feelings and physical reactions similar to those of their patients, or experiencing emotions and behaviors their clients may be blocking or split off from. Further, analysts use principles of projective identification to guide their therapeutic reactions. Therefore, it is not possible (or sensible) to write a book on vicarious trauma and emotional contagion—theories that also endeavor to understand these same phenomena—without paying attention to projective identification.

While projective identification is a cornerstone of psychoanalysis, there is a good deal of professional disagreement regarding its existence, what it is and is not, how it occurs, and whether it is useful or harmful. In this section, the history of projective identification and its current status are discussed. In Chapter 5 the concept is revisited. There I take a critical look at it in light of the new theories, concepts, and procedures discussed in the pages between.

History of the Concept

Projective identification was first introduced to psychoanalysis by Melanie Klein (1946). She saw it as a primitive mental phenomenon, a form of communication that could occur in any interpersonal relationship, beginning in the contact between an infant and its primary caregiver. Basically, it involves the projection of parts of the self onto—or into—another person.

Klein believed that an infant is not psychologically equipped to identify its own emotional states as something occurring within its tiny being. Instead, it "projects" those states "into" the mother or other primary caretaker. (As the caretaker is usually the mother, for shorthand, I will refer to "mother.") As a result, the infant perceives the mother as the cause of its emotions, believing that they originate outside of the infant's self. This trend can persist through life as the child, and later the adult, continues to project those states and traits that it does not like or cannot accept in itself onto others. Klein and her followers believe that an individual—infant, child, or adult—puts those states, those emotions, into the other person. When projective identification occurs in the psychoanalytic relationship, it becomes the analyst's job to process the projections and give them back to the patient in a more palatable form.

The notion that unwanted emotions can be put into another person appears to be the major difference between Klein's idea of projective identification and Anna Freud's (1937) earlier concept of projection. In basic projection, the unwanted emotions are perceived as being a part of the other, whether or not that person is expressing them. Denying your own anger while accusing your spouse of being angry with you would be a common example of Anna Freud's projection. Klein's projective identification would instead suggest that you put your feelings of anger into your spouse because you will not feel them or cannot identify yourself as an angry person. Your spouse then becomes angry with you, seemingly for no reason. In Klein's view, the angry spouse is not feeling his own feelings, that is, becoming angry as a reasonable or unreasonable reaction to the situation. In essence, Klein believed you unconsciously make your spouse feel and act out your anger. In the psychoanalytic relationship, it is the client who is believed to unconsciously put uncomfortable, unwanted, and disowned feelings into the analyst. Further, as a result, the analyst may be "induced" by the client to behave in certain ways, such as acting angrily toward him. When the client is dealing with traumatic events, vicarious traumatization may be viewed as inducing the therapist to feel the horror of the trauma.

Grotstein (1981) made a major contribution to the theory of projective identification by identifying psychological *splitting* as a major component. For projective identification to be possible, he believed at least one member of a relationship (infant, child, adult) has to split his or her perception of the self, as well as his or her perception of the other, into good and bad aspects, disavowing or splitting off one of those aspects.

The next step requires an unconscious fantasy of projecting the split-off aspect into the other. An example may help to clarify this complicated process: When an infant's distress cannot be alleviated by his mother, he may feel himself to be bad—"I'm inconsolable, so I must be a bad baby." Since feeling bad about oneself is not a comfortable feeling, the infant may project that perception of "badness" onto his mother, believing her to be bad because she cannot calm him. When the infant is calmed, he then perceives himself as a good baby, and also projects that perception onto his, now, good mother—"She is able to care for me." Mother may or may not be conscious of this process. The mother who remains confident in her ability to eventually calm her child will not be caught up in whether she is a good or bad mother. She will know that sometimes baby calming takes more time, sometimes less time. However, if she is anxious and self-critical, she may split her perception of herself and her baby as well: "I'm a bad mother and he's a bad baby"; "He's a fussy baby, so I must be a bad mother"; or "He makes me feel like a bad mother." Healing such splits involves a realistic appraisal of distressing situations. For the child that means eventually realizing, "Sometimes mother can calm me quickly, sometimes it takes longer; sometimes she does not know what I need." Likewise, it is useful for the mother to accept that sometimes she may need help to care for her child and that she will not always be able to assess her baby's needs accurately or satisfy every one of them.

Bion (1959) helped us to understand the above example. He believed that the infant projects negative emotional states and unwanted impulses into the mother. She then absorbs, contains, neutralizes, or somehow transforms those feelings. If the mother can contain and transform the feelings and is not harmed by them, the infant feels safe. The effect of this process on the developing infant depends on the ability of the mother to manage the negative projection. Applied to the example above, if the crying infant does not arouse anxiety in the mother, she will then be able to calm him, making his perception of both himself and his mother good. To the extent that the mother may not be able to tolerate these projected feeling states, then bad or dangerous aspects will not be contained and transformed by her and will remain in the infant as a negative introjection of both itself and its mother (Hedges, 1983). This turns the mother into a frightening or, at the very least, an unreliable person.

Intrapsychic or Intersubjective

A primitive mental mechanism throughout life, projective identification replicates the elemental process between caretaker and infant in other relationships, including the therapeutic relationship. Projective identification was thought by Klein (1957) to be an interpersonal, intersubjective process. Grotstein (1981) disagreed with Klein, proposing that projective identification is intrapsychic. He believed the projection is directed at an internalized image of the mother (or other in a relationship, e.g., the therapist), not into the actual mother (or other). "I do not project into objects [people] in the external world; I project into my image of them. If my objects are in an intimate state of correspondence with us, they may be on a 'shortwave' frequency and respond keenly to desires and wishes" (Grotstein, 1981, p. 133).

Contemporary relational theorists use an interpersonal definition of projective identification in which the infant's intrapsychic activity determines not only its own emotional experiences but those of the mother as well (Stolorow, Atwood, & Orange, 2002). This view fits with Schore's (1994) definition of projective identification. He saw it as the unconscious interaction of two minds and believed that it involves nonverbal communication. Schore also proposed that projective identification may provide a bridge between the intrapsychic and the interpersonal.

According to Grotstein (1981) and Kohut (1959, 1971), projective identification may form the basis for empathy. Intersubjective theory originated in Kohut's work on empathy (discussed in the next section). He believed that the client projects missing functions of the self (soothing, calming, understanding, etc.) onto the therapist, and the therapist then provides those functions for the client until the client can integrate and perform them himself. From this viewpoint, projective identification facilitates a therapist's empathetic understanding of the client's needs.

The view of Stolorow and colleagues (2002) is that projective identification is an interpersonal process rooted in affect attunement: The caretaker and baby are able to regulate one another's affective states nonverbally and unconsciously. Affect attunement is in evidence when the baby's state of distress is soothed merely by proximity to the calm mother, or when the mother accurately senses the baby's need (for contact, feeding, change of diaper, etc.). Such a result from affect attunement is seen in the therapeutic relationship often, as when the anxious client becomes calm in the therapist's presence. Some of our clients call our voice mail for the same reason: Just hearing the therapist's voice can be calming. Stolorow and his colleagues (2002) refuted the classical interpretation of projective identification. He questioned the belief that one can induce a visceral change or behavior in another, as, for example, the client causing the therapist to feel or do something specific. He saw this as a confusion of psychological (subjective) and physical (objective) interaction.

Projective Identification in the Therapeutic Relationship

Psychoanalysis utilizes an integrated, if complicated, application of projective identification. Martha Stark's (1999) *Modes of Therapeutic Action* has excellent in-depth examples of this process in action. In the hands of an adept analyst, the principle of projective identification may facilitate healing in a psychoanalytic patient. However, when it is not well understood, in the hands of the less experienced, or applied generally within other types of therapeutic models or therapeutic relationships, it can become problematic. While it originated in psychoanalysis, the theory of projective identification has been widely, if sometimes inaccurately, adopted

by many other disciplines. The consequence can be therapists blaming or holding their clients responsible for their
own uncomfortable feelings, for example, "My client wouldn't
feel her anger, so I ended up with it." Usually, psychoanalysts
regard projective identification as a normal and desirable part
of the psychoanalytic process. Some analysts, however, as
well as many psychotherapists from other disciplines, view
projective identification as something that detracts from, or
even harms, the therapeutic relationship. Outside of psychoanalysis, it is often regarded as an inconvenient or undesirable
defense mechanism associated with psychopathology and
early developmental trauma (Grotstein, 1981).

Many believe that projective identification holds the power
to provoke countertransference in the practitioner. In this
view, nearly all negative and positive feelings toward a client
may be disowned by the therapist as being caused by the client
(Hedges, 1983). This tendency can be very problematic, not
just because of the risk of hurting the client. The therapist who
is unable to distinguish her own feelings from those of her
client, and who also feels at the mercy of her client's feelings,
may increase her risk for compassion fatigue, vicarious traumatization, unmanageable countertransference, and burnout.

The case example of Bobbe (see p. 19) can be used to illustrate and contrast some of the differences between countertransference and projective identification. If you will remember (or review), with the help of her supervisor, Bobbe
discovered her feelings had roots in her own high school history. Projective identification could be another possible interpretation for the same situation—particularly if Bobbe
were unable to find (or unwilling to look for) a link in her
own past. Then it would be easy to interpret her harsh reaction toward her client as being induced by the client's unconscious rejection of her own feelings of harshness toward
others. If Bobbe is on the right track, that could be helpful
to the client. But if she is on the wrong track, such an interpretation could be detrimental for them both.

Schore (1994) speculated that projective identification is relevant to empathy, the topic of Chapter 2. Perhaps it is even more than that: Maybe projective identification is empathy, or a category of empathy, something that the therapist tunes into rather than something that happens to him. Theories that support such a premise are discussed throughout the rest of this book. In Chapter 5, I take another look at projective identification, with the additional insights developed through the intervening chapters. By then the reader should be well equipped to understand—and take charge of—the mechanisms underlying those shared feelings and states that regularly occur in the therapeutic relationship.

EMPATHY

The only area of agreement in the literature on empathy is that there is wide disagreement about what empathy is. This disagreement also extends to the concept of sympathy. In many articles and books, *sympathy* and *empathy* are virtually interchangeable terms standing for the same concept. Others, however, make a clear distinction between the two. In nearly every article and book on the topic, both terms are subject to differing definitions. For the purposes of this book, I have decided to depend on the definition of empathy in *Merriam-Webster's Collegiate Dictionary*:

> The action of understanding, being aware of, being sensitive to, and vicariously experiencing the feelings, thoughts, and experience of another of either the past or present without having the feelings, thoughts, and experience fully communicated in an objectively explicit manner. (1996, p. 378)

Empathy is necessary for survival of the species. It is what alerts us to the needs of others and draws us to respond. Empathy is the foremost tool in the hands of every psychotherapist. None of us would have much success without our capacity and facility for empathy.

Empathy also triggers gut sensations that can advise us who can be trusted and who should be feared. Conscious empathy is a desirable capacity, making it possible for us to relate to the experiences of others, to "walk in their shoes," so to speak. It is part and parcel of being human. Empathy leads to compassion by giving us insight into another's state of being. "I know how you feel" is a common expression of empathy.

However, empathy also has a downside, particularly when it is not conscious and is therefore beyond one's ability to moderate. When, as proposed in the definition above, one is vicariously experiencing the state of another unconsciously, there can be a strong emotional and somatic impact. A common, if benign, example could go as follows. Judy says to her husband at dinner, "No, I did not have an enjoyable lunch. My colleague, Susan, was in a funk and it really got to me. I felt badly for her and tried to help. But when we parted she was still upset, and I've felt lousy all afternoon." Obviously Judy was trying to be a good friend. So why did she end up suffering too? Before answering this question, a look at the roots of the concept of empathy is in order.

The History of Empathy

As I began to peruse the existing literature in research for this book, I assumed that the idea of empathy was a theory exclusive to psychology. Actually, it is not. I was surprised to learn that the notion of empathy was first applied in the context of art appreciation. In the late 19th and early 20th centuries, empathy was considered essential to understanding aesthetics, the idea that a person could be deeply affected by the mood of something else—a painting, a sculpture— and the term *empathy* was applied to that effect. The earliest writings on the topic appear from Theodor Lipps (1903/ 1964) who, in German, used the term *Einfühlung* to name the kinds of feelings that could be noticed in the body, including proprioceptive changes and sensations.

Since the early 1900s, psychologists from a variety of disciplines, including social psychology, neurophysiology, and folk psychology, have studied empathy. Though empathy has been studied for decades, many of the early findings were not always taken seriously. Prior to the Decade of the Brain in the 1990s, psychology was often considered a soft science, its research not readily accepted. New technologies, including various types of brain scanning, are turning the field of psychology into an accepted hard science. However, empathy remains an elusive and complicated concept, even for psychotherapists.

There is no better resource on the early history of empathy than Gladstein's (1984) "The Historical Roots of Contemporary Empathy Research." Reviewed below are some of the most salient points from that article, interspersed with a few additional points from other sources.

The earliest definitions of empathy were anthropomorphic; that is, *empathy* referred to people infusing objects and art with human qualities (Gladstein, 1984). By the late 19th and early 20th centuries, this view was superseded by an interpersonal view of empathy. While E. B. Titchener coined the actual term *empathy* in 1909, it appears he based it on Theodor Lipps's (1903/1964) earlier concept of *Einfühlung*.

Some researchers began to notice an interpersonal element to empathy. The contagious nature of laughter is one example. "Emotional contagion" (MacDougall, 1908) and "fellow-feeling" (Scheler, 1912) were terms coined to describe the effect of inter-personal empathy. Sullivan (1947, 1954) observed that a child quickly picked up the tension of an anxious mother and called it "contagion of emotion." Others soon added to these basic observations.

Applications of empathy in psychotherapy slowly evolved through the middle of the 20th century. In 1948, Theodor Reik wrote, "the analyst must oscillate in the same rhythm with his patient. He vicariously lives his patient's experiences and at the same time looks upon them with the factual regard of the investigator" (p. 116). Similarly, Carl Rogers (1946) suggested that the therapist should use "deep understanding" and try to perceive the client "as the client seems to himself." By 1951, Rogers had begun using the terms *empathic attitude* and *empathic understanding* in his discussion of the counselor-client relationship. Heinz Kohut (1978), the psychoanalyst who founded the movement of self-psychology, believed that the field of psychology itself should be defined by the concept of empathy.

Kohut's Empathy

As recently as the 1970s, new ground was still being broken in the discovery of the importance of empathy in all types of interpersonal relationships, including the therapeutic relationship. Leading that charge was Heinz Kohut. He regarded the healthy functioning of the self (for our purposes, the therapist) in relation to others (clients) to be of primary importance if empathy is to be effective. Even though Kohut first introduced his concepts of empathy in 1959, he did not break away from classical psychoanalysis until 1971, when he published *The Analysis of the Self*.

Kohut believed that classical psychoanalysis failed to help patients who had pre-oedipal (before 3 years of age) trauma. He found that interpretation and insight alone did not help such patients to feel understood. He set out to develop a therapeutic method that involved verbal reflection (as opposed to psychoanalytic interpretation) of the client's subjective experience. His aim was to help the client to feel understood. Kohut's concept of empathy relies on the comprehension of another's experience from that person's perspective. The idea is to get a sense of how it feels to be in the other person's shoes. Kohut found that when he was successful in understanding what the client was feeling and could demonstrate his understanding through accurate verbal reflection, his patient would improve. Kohut believed that empathy and verbal reflection were necessary keys for addressing early developmental deficiencies.

Empathy in the Therapeutic Relationship

In the earlier example, I asked: Why, when Judy was trying to be helpful, did she end up suffering along with her friend? Here is one possible answer: Judy was unaware that she took on so much of Susan's feelings and that her empathy could have consequences. As a result, she was infected by Susan's upset without having the tools to identify or intervene in that automatic process.

Unconscious empathy is the mechanism of emotional infection. This is the same mechanism that is at work on a regular basis in the therapeutic relationship: Therapists commonly "catch" the upset feelings of their clients. Often the effect is short-lived. But sometimes the impact is lasting, persisting long after the end of a session. If, for example, you find yourself feeling down during or following work with a depressed client, or hungry during or after a session with an anorexic client, empathy may be the culprit. Of course, empathy is very important in the therapeutic relationship and is by no means always a problem.

About 20 minutes into one session, Lillian, a marriage and family therapist, gained an important insight into the plight of her client Isaac. He was struggling with an irrational anger toward authority figures that had caused problems at his workplace. Frankly, Lillian was somewhat irritated with him, thinking he should have better impulse control. And she was frustrated that she was unable to get him to think more clearly. But today, as Isaac ranted about a coworker, Lillian flashed on a surprisingly similar conversation she'd recently had with her 8-year-old son. He had come home crying after being rebuffed by another child. Of course, many of the particulars were different, but the feelings and themes were similar. When she made that link, that Isaac was feeling and responding as her young son would, her feelings toward him softened and her irritation receded. She could now see underneath his anger and resonate with his unexpressed hurt feelings. As a result, she felt more in contact with him, not so antagonistic. Lillian then changed her tactics and began to talk with Isaac as she would with her son, to that young part of him. For the first time in several sessions, they really connected. Isaac felt heard and supported, and he calmed down. That made it possible for him to look at the situation with his coworker differently. Both Lillian and Isaac felt good at the end of this successful session.

This example illustrates one of the ways in which empathy can be a critically useful tool for the psychotherapist. Lillian tapped into her own memory and feelings for a link to Isaac. When they connected, she was better able to help him. Lillian was aware of the link and the change in her feelings. The session left no residue in her system. However, empathy's mark is not always so positive.

Hans was a psychologist at a refugee assistance center. Though he had never been homeless or displaced himself, he still had a deep empathy for his clients. Of course, sometimes this facilitated his work with them. But over time, his energy began to flag and his optimism faltered. Empathy with a particular client accelerated Hans toward the edge of burnout. He had been working with Kabil for about 6 months. Kabil had fled his Middle Eastern country during a political upheaval. Like many of Hans's clients, Kabil had been in mortal danger because of views that were sympathetic to the previous regime. He was forced to leave family and friends behind to settle in Hans's country once he was granted refugee status. Typical of many refugees, Kabil was depressed and greatly missed his home country, family, and friends. The therapy sessions were often laden with sadness and frustration.

*Hans was greatly affected by Kabil's feelings. If Hans had
been able to observe one of these sessions, he would have
been surprised by what he saw. Invariably, as he listened
intently, he would gradually slip into deeper and deeper
resonance with Kabil. It was easily observable, not only in
Hans's demeanor, but also in his posture, his breathing,
and his facial expression. His empathy was so deep that
for the duration of a session, Hans was, in essence, one
with Kabil. Of course this deep affinity provided Kabil
with a very sympathetic ear. But there was a disadvan-
tage: Hans was losing his ability to be objectively helpful, and feelings of hopelessness and depression were beginning to spill into his private life. His wife was
becoming concerned. By resonating so deeply (and unconsciously) with Kabil (and other clients), Hans was losing the optimism he needed to help improve Kabil's life, as
well as to live his own.*

Summary

Empathy is a multifaceted evolutionary phenomenon that facilitates the binding of people to each other. Knowing what
another is feeling or feeling the same emotion oneself is a
result of empathy. This ability has played a major role in the
development of humankind by making it possible for individuals to bond into couples and groups, and to care for and
socialize their young. Empathy appears to be incredibly useful, truly at the root of the survival of the human species. It
also seems to have some disadvantages, as Judy and Hans
would attest. In Chapter 2, the neurobiology of empathy,
this mechanism that binds humans to each other, is explored
and skills are offered to both enhance the benefits and interrupt the risks of empathy between therapist and client.

Chapter 2
Managing the Ties That Bind

W hat are the mechanisms of both body and brain that underlie the phenomenon of empathy? The theory section of this chapter will strive to answer that question by exploring the neurophysiology of empathy, the distinct features of somatic empathy, and the inevitable human tendency for mirroring and mimicry. In the skill building section, the reader will be taught to increase mindfulness and control over facial and postural awareness, and to engage in both conscious postural mirroring and unmirroring.

THEORY
The Neurophysiology of Empathy

This section illuminates the neurophysiology that makes it possible to vicariously feel what another person is feeling (as illustrated by Hans at the end of the previous chapter). To be able to understand how such a feat is possible, it is first necessary to be familiar with some basics of human nervous system structure and function.

The term *central nervous system* (CNS) commonly has two usages. The first is (incorrectly) as the name of the body's entire nervous system. More accurately, however, the term describes that portion of the nervous system that is most central in the body: the brain and spinal cord. It is from that core that all of the body's nerves emanate.

The nerves of the CNS first connect the brain and spinal cord. From there they distribute to all points in the body as the *peripheral nervous system*. Nerves communicate throughout the body via hormones, *neurotransmitters*, that facilitate the transfer of information across *synapses*, the junctions between nerve endings. *Efferent nerves* transmit instructions from the brain to the body (e.g., "Contract the left flexor digiti minimi brevis," to bend the little finger of the left hand). *Afferent nerves* broadcast sensory information from the body to the brain (e.g., "Moving that finger hurts"). Grasping the basics of this two-way system is integral to understanding the vicarious nature of empathy: the brain communicates to the body *and* the body communicates back to the brain. More on this later.

The peripheral nervous system has two divisions: sensory and motor. They each also have two divisions. The motor (muscle) division is divided into somatic and autonomic branches, and the sensory division is divided into *exteroceptor* and *interoceptor* branches (see Figure 2.1). In Chapter 3, the motor division's autonomic nervous system (ANS) is discussed in depth. This chapter focuses on the somatic nervous system and both branches of the sensory division: interoceptive and exteroceptive.

Motor Division: Somatic Nervous System

The nerves of the body's skeletal muscles comprise the somatic nervous system. Stimulation to one of these nerves

FIGURE 2.1 THE STRUCTURE OF THE HUMAN NERVOUS SYSTEM

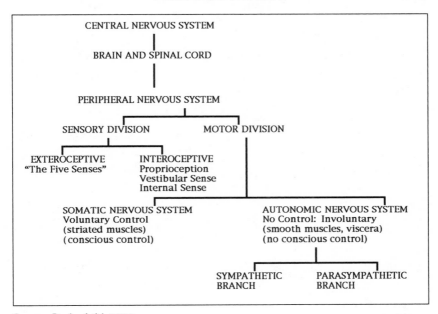

Source: Rothschild, 2000.

causes it to contract; in the absence of stimulation, there is no contraction. Nothing happens in the muscle. The common term for this nonaction or noncontraction is *relaxation*, which sounds like an active process ("just relax!"), though it is not. It is the contractions and noncontractions of a muscle, regulated from the brain or spinal cord, that create physical movement.

The somatic nervous system is composed of efferent nerves, which carry instructions from the brain and spinal cord to the muscles. For example, when your eyes move to follow the printed text in this book, your brain must signal nerves to stimulate muscles on one side of your eyes to contract. At the same time, there must also be a signal to nerves on the opposite side of your eyes to stop stimulation so that those muscles do nothing (relax). As your eyes sweep from left to right, muscles on the right side of the eyeball are contracting while the ones on the left side are releasing. It is this interplay of contraction and release that makes the eye movement (or any movement) possible. When your eyes sweep back to the left, the opposite is happening. If you are wearing progressive eyeglasses, it will not be your eyes that are moving, but your head that is turning from side to side as you read. In that case, it will be muscles at the sides of the neck that are alternately contracting and releasing to make possible the head movement that facilitates reading. The commands from the brain to the muscles of the eyes or neck travel along efferent nerves, brain to body.

On rare occasions, efferent nerves in the spinal cord can instruct body movement without a directive from the brain. The quick jerk your arm and hand make in reaction to inadvertently touching a hot stove (set in motion by sensory feedback from your fingers or hand) is an example. That instantaneous reflex, yanking your hand out of danger, is directed from the spinal cord; the brain is bypassed. As can be seen from this and later examples, the sensory and motor divisions of the nervous system interact all the time. In fact, without sensory feedback, successful movement is not even possible. Think about trying to walk without being able to feel the bottom of your foot or the weight of your body on your knees.

Sensory Division: Exteroceptors

Sensory nerves are afferent nerves. They are constantly communicating information from the body's periphery to the brain and spinal cord. There are two main categories: exteroceptors and interoceptors. Exteroceptors are nerves that relay the sensory information with which we are most familiar—sight, hearing, taste, touch, smell—what are commonly called the five senses. Communication of exteroceptive nerves connects us to our external environment. In the previous example, it is the exteroceptive sense of touch that is activated by contact with the hot stove.

No single branch of the nervous system functions independently. Information from the sensory nervous system will often generate activity in the somatic nervous system. Continuing with the example above will clarify this interplay: The sensation of endangering heat is quickly communicated to the spinal cord (afferent), where the instruction to contract hand and arm muscles (to jerk the hand away) is sent immediately in response (efferent). A split second or two later, as the sensation of pain reaches the brain (an afferent process that is much slower), further instructions are sent from the brain (efferent), which result in additional muscular movements: shaking the hand, blowing on the fingers, dashing to the freezer to get ice, and so forth.

Sensory Division: Interoceptors

Though it is equally important, most people are less familiar with the interoceptive branch of the sensory nervous system. It comprises three main senses:

- *Vestibular:* regulates your sense of balance, including the relationship of the body to gravity
- *Proprioceptive:* tells you where the parts of your body (including head, trunk, and limbs) are in space at any time
- *Internal:* communicates information about the state of your organs and connective tissue (butterflies in the stomach, muscle aches, etc.)

Proprioception is sometimes a difficult concept to grasp. Two simple exercises will give you a clearer understanding of your body's proprioceptive sense.

- Right now, before looking, identify the position of your legs and feet. Include the angle of each and the proximity of one to the other. Once you have an idea, look and see if you are correct.
- Put on some music and dance a little. Stop suddenly

and, before looking, identify how your legs, feet, arms, hands, head, and so on are positioned (in front of or behind your trunk, bent or straight, tilted or upright, etc.). If you do this with others, ask for their feedback. If you are doing this alone, it can help to check in a mirror.

Like the exteroceptors, the interoceptors also interact with (and influence) other divisions of the nervous system. The nerves of the somatic nervous system, discussed above, do not act alone in moving our bodies around in space. To walk across a room, for instance, requires a cooperative effort across several divisions of the nervous system:

- Somatic nerves contract (and release) the muscles of the legs to facilitate movement and to hold the trunk and head upright.
- Proprioceptive nerves send feedback to the brain on where the legs and feet are in relationship to the body and the floor.
- Vestibular nerves tell the brain whether or not the body is upright.
- The exteroceptive sense of touch communicates the feel of the foot's contact with the floor and the weight of the body on ankle and knee joints.

The internal sense is the core of neurologist Antonio Damasio's theory of somatic markers (1994). He proposed that the experience of emotion consists of "gut" sensations that are elicited in response to various stimuli, including the stimuli of empathy. For example, if you eat something that makes you ill, the next time you see, smell, or are offered it, you may feel some degree of nausea (an internal sensation that has become a somatic marker for the previous experience with that food). After a time the strongest reaction will likely fade, but you may continue to have an involuntary aversion to that food (the somatic marker), perhaps even forgetting the origin of your dislike.

Empathy and the Nervous System

Individuals in close interaction with others (including psychotherapists) commonly, spontaneously, and unconsciously copy each other's facial expressions and postures (as demonstrated by Hans in Chapter 1). Reflexive smiling in response to another's smile is just one example of this. When facial expressions associated with particular emotions are copied, both people may experience the same feeling. This tendency is rooted in afferent feedback from the internal sense and is related to Damasio's somatic marker theory. This idea is expanded in the next two sections, Somatic Empathy and Mirroring and Mimicry.

- Try turning down the sides of your mouth, lowering the outer edges. At the same time, notice what happens in your gut. Do you feel any sensation there? What about any changes in your breathing or sensations in your chest? Do you associate those sensations with a particular feeling?

Many people who try this exercise will sense a kind of heaviness in their gut or chest and will associate it with the feeling of sadness. That is the result of the somatic marker we all have for how sadness feels, both on the face (proprioceptive awareness of my downturned mouth) and in the gut. It is because of this feedback system (à la Damasio's somatic markers) that adopting an empathic facial expression or posture with your client—consciously or unconsciously—can dramatically affect you.

Empathy can also be set in motion by any part of the sensory nervous system. Visual, auditory, and tactile senses are particularly vulnerable. It is commonplace to visualize stories in the mind's eye or hear dialogue in the mind's ear when reading or listening to stories—whether from literature, news (written and broadcast), or direct communication with another. Provocations can also occur in other senses, such as touch when you feel cold observing or hearing about a snowstorm, or taste when you see a cooking show on television or listen to the description of a scrumptious meal. Just as Lipps (1903/1964) found that viewing a painting could stir empathy, so can exposure to other types of sensory stimuli.

Here is another exercise to try: Think of a piece of favorite music from your college years (for this, I often call up songs by The Beatles or Simon and Garfunkel). Listen to it in your imagination (or put it on the stereo) and notice what happens in your sensory system. Do you have memories of smells, tastes, movements, etc. from the time that you most listened to that music?

For another experience, imagine your spice rack and remember the smell of each spice, one at a time. Alternatively, you can try actually smelling the spices. Notice if pictures arise in your mind's eye or sensations in your mouth or stomach in association with your memories of the different fragrances.

Once you have experienced this firsthand, it will be easier to comprehend how listening to and observing a client could elicit sensory material in yourself.

THE NEUROLOGY OF EMPATHY

Neuroscience is attempting to explain the interpersonal phenomena of imitation, resonance, simulation, and the somatoemotional results of those processes that are called empathy. Promising new theories have come from the mid-1990s discovery of what are now called *mirror neurons*.

Mirror neurons are just what their name implies: brain cells that reflect the activity of another's brain cells. They were first discovered by Italian researchers (Gallese, Fadiga, Fogassi, & Rizzolatti, 1996; Rizzolatti, Fadiga, Gallese, & Fogassi, 1996) at Universitá Degli Studi di Parma (the University of Parma). Actually, the discovery was accidental—a common occurrence in the evolution of scientific ideas.

These researchers were studying grasping behaviors in live monkeys. They observed activity in the monkeys' brains via electrodes connected to a monitor, so they could identify which neurons were firing at any given time. Specifically, they were investigating which individual neurons fired when a monkey reached out and grasped a raisin. During a break, something amazing—and never before detected—happened with one of the primate subjects: Neurons in the monkey's brain associated with grasping lit up when one of the *researchers* reached out and grasped a raisin (Gallese, 1999). That is, *the neurons that fired when the monkey itself grasped a raisin were the exact same ones that fired when the monkey* observed *the researcher's similar grasping movement*. The same neuron activated by performing the action was also activated by *seeing* the action.

Of course the researchers were amazed. Nothing like this had been seen before. There had been some previous speculation about a motor matching system (Fadiga, Fogassi, Pavesi, & Rizzolatti, 1995), but proof had not yet been observed. In this case, the neurons in the monkey's motor system were actually observed responding to the action of the researcher. Through that simple grasping movement, the monkey and the researcher essentially became connected to one another. Rizzolatti and Arbib proposed that mirror neurons "represent the link between sender and receiver" (1998, p. 188). For an action to elicit the response of mirror neurons, it must be seen (or perhaps imagined) in process. The visual stimulus of the actor activates the same neurons in the observer (Gallese, 2001).

This accidental occurrence was the first evidence for the existence of a neuronal mirror system, meaning that the monkey might *feel* the researcher's movement. The mirror response in the monkey's neurons was not just simple recognition, the monkey's awareness of what the researcher was doing. That kind of thoughtful perception is activated elsewhere in the brain. What happened between the monkey and the researcher necessitated a new concept, a new theory. The monkey's neurons fired *as if it had made the same movement itself*. Actually, our bodies frequently recognize another's movement; it just had not been documented in the brain before. You have probably experienced the same thing yourself—a time you cringed when seeing someone get hurt, or felt your thighs tense or your breathing accelerate while you were watching sports or a passionate love scene on television.

Renowned neuroscientist V.S. Ramachandran (2000) voiced extreme excitement at the discovery of mirror neurons. He enthusiastically predicted that mirror neurons could revolutionize psychology in a manner similar to DNA's revolution of biology. Ramachandran speculated that phenomena such as ESP—which has stumped scientists for eons—could be explained by mirror neurons.

Usually discussed within the context of observation and imitation of movement, including the development of spoken language, mirror neurons actually appear to be involved in many more areas of the brain and many more aspects of interaction. The role of mirror neurons in language development is simple to grasp (pun intended) as it likely underpins the evolution of human communication, beginning with gesticular language. It has been shown, for example, that Broca's area, the major center for the production of speech in humans, is also important for the production of gestures (Chollet et al., 1991; Parsons et al., 1995). Moreover, several studies have observed a mirror response to hand gestures in the neurons of Broca's area (Arbib et al., 2000; Rizzolatti & Arbib, 1998). This implies that communication among humans was likely dependent on gesture in earlier times. Moreover, modern day language development in children often includes sign language. For example, toddlers are able to point at something they want long before they are able to express their desire in words.

International travelers also know, firsthand, the importance of gesture in communication. How many of us have found our way in a foreign land by depending on sign language? Finding a place in a strange city can be almost always be facilitated by stating the name of the place you are looking for while simultaneously raising your shoulders with hands upturned—connecting a place name with that gesture is universally understood as asking where it is.

From these beginnings, interest in mirror neurons has grown rapidly. Scientists are now looking at mirror neurons as a possible explanation for common phenomena. For example, it is possible that mirror neurons will help us understand the obvious infectiousness of laughter and yawning. Platek and colleagues (2003) conducted several experiments on the contagiousness of yawning. Among other things, their data suggested that yawning is a kind of empathic response quite possibly mediated by mirror neurons. They are not the only ones to study and to speculate about the relationship between empathy and mirror neurons. A growing body of literature focuses on that very idea including: Cozolino, 2002; Decety & Chaminade, 2003; Gallese, 2001; Harris, 2003; Preston & de Waal, 2002; Wolf et al., 2000; Wolf, Gales, Shane, & Shane, 2001.

Somatic Empathy

Empathy is deeply grounded in the experience of my lived-body, and it is this experience that enables us to directly recognize others, not as bodies endowed with a mind, but as *persons* like us.
—*Gallese, Ferrari, and Umilta* (2002)

[Empathy is] an autonomic nervous system state which tends to simulate that of another person.
—*Ax* (1964)

A situation that occurred in my first job as a new social worker in the mid-1970s will help to illustrate how vulnerable we are to being infected by the states of our clients.

While I sat in my office with particular clients, I would observe things happening in my body that I did not notice with all clients. The pleasant sensations did not concern me and I did not pay much attention to them. However, I found that I did need to do something about sensations that were not so pleasant. Some of my uncomfortable responses could be blamed on newbie jitters, but I strongly sensed that there was more to it than that. For example, I distinctly remember my bodily reactions to Allison. As she recounted the crises of her week in a spacey, disconnected way, she kept her body very still. I had to lean forward to hear her whispery, nearly inaudible voice. As we worked together, I often noticed that I felt light-headed, which I did not like. When I began to pay attention to what was happening in my body, I found that my breathing had become very shallow—in fact, nearly undetectable. No wonder I was feeling light-headed and spacey. I wasn't getting enough oxygen.

Turning my attention back to Allison, I noticed that her chest was barely moving. I was taken aback—we were breathing alike! Was I copying her respiration style? I wondered if my light-headedness and general feelings of disconnectedness were just the result of new-therapist nervousness or the direct result of my imitation of Allison's breathing? If (as it appeared) our respiration had actually become synchronized, I thought, it was totally unconscious on both our parts.

In all of my graduate school discussions on the therapeutic relationship, including the fine points of transference and countertransference, I couldn't remember anyone ever mentioning the possibility of "catching" bodily behaviors. Intrigued and a bit bewildered, I took my observations to my supervisor. I still remember her look of startled skepticism. "What an odd hypothesis," she finally remarked, her cool tone clearly implying that my experience was not to be taken seriously. I was dumbfounded by her lack of curiosity, but I never doubted my own sensations.

The previous sections highlighted the historic roots and the evolution of the concept of empathy in psychology and the science that may underlie empathy. This chapter takes that concept a step further, demonstrating that empathy is not only a psychological phenomenon but also a physical one.

The following pages highlight a mere fraction of the research that leads to the conclusion that the body is centrally involved in empathy. A surprisingly large quantity of hard scientific evidence indicates that empathy is more than a cognitive process. Empathy is, in fact, a highly integrated process involving both cognitive and somatic, brain and body. The cognitive aspects have been studied at length and are fairly well known, as discussed previously. The somatic side, how empathy is communicated and expressed through the body and from one body to another, is less well known. Neuroscience is the latest entrant into the study of empathy. This discussion includes previous as well as new areas of research that appear to have promise in helping us to further understand how the body, mind, and brain interact in the phenomenon of empathy.

BODY TO BODY

Most of us automatically smile when another smiles at us. It is a normal human response that may have nothing to do with whether or not we know the other person. Our bodies (in this case, the muscles around our mouths) just respond. Something similar happens when we see someone yawn—it is nearly impossible to stifle a sympathetic yawn. In fact, our bodies respond to other people's bodies all the time. Face-to-face contact is not even necessary. Can you remember the last time you enjoyed a sexy scene in a movie? Your body's response to that scene is an example of somatic empathy.

Freud's original ideas about conversion hysteria were among the first psychological theories to recognize the relationship between mind and body. Wilhelm Reich, one of Freud's most famous (and infamous) students, went off on his own tack to further Freud's early somatic theories and to develop *Orgonomy*, a mind-body integrated approach to treating mental illness (Reich, 1972). Since then, many well-known models and methods of both psychotherapy and body psychotherapy have given attention to the interconnectedness of mind and body (including bioenergetics, gestalt, cognitive behavioral, somatic experiencing, body-mind psychotherapy, and eye movement desensitization and reprocessing). However, while psychological theories of empathy have existed for a long time, it is only recently that the body has been acknowledged as a significant player in the phenomenon of empathy.

Early on the scene were Elaine Hatfield and her colleagues at the University of Hawaii (Hsee, Hatfield, Carlson, & Chemtob, 1990). Hatfield became interested in how people seemed to catch the emotions of others and called the phenomenon *emotional contagion*. While the term had been used by others in a few previous articles (Gladstein, 1984; Schoenewolf, 1990; Stiff, Dillard, & Somera, 1988), it was Hatfield and her colleagues who fully developed the concept (Hatfield, Cacioppo, & Rapson, 1994). Emotional contagion differs from previous definitions of empathy by identifying it as a circumstance of shared feelings. That is, in emotional contagion, I feel what you feel; I have "caught it." Pertinent to the thesis of this book, Hatfield acknowledged the body as a central vehicle for emotional contagion. Her theory includes the hypothesis that facial, vocal, and postural mimicry are centrally involved. The result of emotional contagion is a convergence of one person's emotions with another's (Hatfield, Cacioppo, & Rapson, 1992). Further, Hatfield believed that emotional contagion is an inevitable consequence of human interaction. Beginning with the next theory section, Mirroring and Mimicry, I argue (and teach skills to demonstrate) that we can actually easily learn to choose whether or not we are infected by another's feelings. But first the theory of somatic empathy needs to be clarified.

DEVELOPING THE CONCEPT OF SOMATIC EMPATHY

The best term to describe the bodily aspects of empathy is *somatic empathy*. To make the idea of somatic empathy easily understood, it will be useful to disassemble and track the elements that led me to the concept. Each point is then briefly discussed individually, supported with validating scientific studies. The most salient topics are expanded in their own chapter sections. First, it is helpful to distinguish three terms.

In English, *emotion* and *feeling* are nearly interchangeable. Many have endeavored to distinguish them, but none of the distinctions has really caught on. To date, Damasio has been the most successful. Through all three of his books (Damasio, 1994, 1999, 2003), he proposed a very useful differentiation between emotion and feeling. According to him, *emotion* includes all things body: sensations, autonomic and somatic muscular changes, movement, and so forth. *Feeling*, on the other hand, is the label that describes the summation of these body states once they are recognized by the mind. So a feeling is the cortex's name for an experience of emotion. Next time you identify that you are sad, angry, happy, take a minute to notice the bodily sensations and muscular tensions that underlie that *feeling*. For example, when angry, you might identify tension in your shoulders or jaw, and heat in your face. According to Damasio, those are exactly what comprise emotion. Damasio (1999) proposed that *affect* is a more general term covering the topic that includes emotions and feelings.

There is a logical progression to understanding the veracity of the existence of somatic empathy. Actually, the necessary research exists in diverse areas, but no one as yet has pulled all the elements together. This nine-point progressive argument is summarized and then discussed in detail below.

1. Each feeling (happy, sad, angry, surprised, afraid, etc.) has a specific, observable somatic manifestation:

facial expression and body posture (or movement) achieved through a distribution of muscular tension and relaxation.

2. Every feeling has a particular pattern of nonobservable activity associated with it: Autonomic nervous system (ANS) changes in heart rate, skin temperature, and so forth.

3. The observable characteristics of facial expression and posture can be consciously copied (mimicked or mirrored) voluntarily, muscle by muscle.

4. Copying the muscular changes associated with a particular feeling induces the associated ANS reactions. One body intentionally empathizes with the other.

5. Muscle patterns also can be (and often are) imitated unconsciously. During normal situations of interpersonal contact, it is common for people to mirror the facial and postural muscular patterns of one another.

6. Unconscious mirroring will also induce associated ANS reactions and feelings. One person is feeling what the other is feeling but does not realize it.

7. Instinctive synchrony of affective and ANS states in others may have an evolutionary role for survival of the species.

8. Sometimes somatic empathy manifests as what seems to be mind reading, intuition, or ESP. However, it can also have negative consequences for the unconscious participant.

9. The activity of the brain's mirror neurons may account for some portion of unconscious mimicry.

Discussion

1. Each feeling (happy, sad, angry, surprised, afraid, etc.) has a specific, observable somatic manifestation: Facial expression and body posture (or movement)

are achieved through a distribution of muscular tension and relaxation.

The commonality of emotional facial expressions has been researched for nearly 150 years. In 1867, Charles Darwin surveyed missionaries and others who were living around the world in different cultures: Aboriginal, Indian, African, Native American, Chinese, Malayan, and Ceylonese. He wanted to find out if affects, as well as their observable expressions, were consistent across various cultures. When visiting each culture, he asked to be shown how individuals looked when angry, sad, happy, and so forth. The results of his survey showed consistency for all ranges of affect across unrelated and often isolated cultures, as well as common somatic expression of those affects (Darwin, 1872/1987). The world over, people smile when happy, frown and shed tears when sad, open mouths wide in surprise, and so on. Since Darwin's ground-breaking study, others have followed suit to demonstrate the universality of emotional expression.

In recent years, Paul Ekman (2003b) has confirmed Darwin's early findings. In 1965, he took photographs of Americans expressing a variety of feelings to an isolated tribe in Papua, New Guinea. He showed the photos to many of the natives—some who had had contact with other cultures, and some who had not. All of the natives were easily able to identify the feelings being expressed in those pictures. This was possible, of course, because the natives in that isolated tribe also expressed their feelings in the same ways.

2. Every feeling has a particular pattern of nonobservable activity associated with it: Autonomic nervous system (ANS) changes in heart rate, skin temperature, respiration, etc. as well as the common physical sensations that are normally associated with feelings.

Again, Paul Ekman and his colleagues are at the forefront of those studying affects and their associated ANS changes. They have conducted studies both in the United States and in West Sumatra, and have found a commonality of ANS changes across cultural bounds (Ekman, Levenson, & Friesen, 1983; Levenson, 1992; Levenson, Ekman, & Friesen, 1990; Levenson, Ekman, & Heider, 1992).

In particular, Ekman and colleagues (1983) were able to demonstrate specific changes in heart rate and skin temperature. They found elevated heart rates for anger, fear, and sadness, and decreased heart rates for happiness, disgust, and surprise. Skin temperature raised the most with anger and lowered the most with fear and sadness.

3. The observable characteristics of facial expression and posture can be consciously copied (mimicked or mirrored) voluntarily, muscle by muscle.

This one you can try for yourself. Together with a friend, partner, or client, mimic as closely as you can the facial expression, posture, or movement of the other. Pay attention to what happens in your own body during each step in the process. Structured mirroring exercises follow in the sections, Mirroring and Mimicry, Facial and Postural Awareness, and Conscious Postural Mirroring.

4. Copying the muscular changes associated with a particular feeling induces the associated ANS reactions. One body intentionally empathizes with another.

Studies in this area are very compelling, as the subjects in most of them had no idea that the researchers were interested in emotions. For instance, Strack, Martin, and Strepper (1988) made subjects simulate a smiling position of the mouth by having them hold a pen between their teeth. When the subjects subsequently read humorous material, they tended to rate it as more amusing than those subjects who had not had their mouths surreptitiously forced into a smile.

Levenson and colleagues (1990) conducted three studies instructing subjects precisely which facial muscles to move and how to move them to replicate specific affects. They found statistically significant correlation between the artificially instructed expressions and the feelings the subjects reported. They further discovered that the subject's ANS responses were consistent with the target emotions. For both results, subjects who were the most precise in their replication of the specific movements or expressions showed the greatest correlations.

Body posture has also been studied. Duclos and associates (1989) instructed subjects in specific postures. Unbeknownst to the subjects, each posture was typical of fear, sadness, or anger. The results clearly demonstrated that emotional postures have an effect on feelings. Duclos concluded that when people copy another's emotional posture, they are more likely to share the same feeling. There is clearly an afferent feedback system (body to brain) from body position and muscle tone that may correspond to Damasio's (1994) concept of somatic markers.

At this writing, together with Dr. Maggie Shiffrar at Rutgers University in New Jersey, I am in the process of conducting studies on postural mirroring and somatic empathy (Rothschild & Shiffrar, 2003, 2004). Our subjects copy the postures of models who are remembering emotionally charged situations from their pasts. Not only do the subjects come to experience many of the same body sensations and feelings, they also are prone to see or hear associated imagery and also often act as mind readers, correctly guessing the situations that were being remembered by the models. Exciting as these preliminary data are, our samples so far have been much too small and variables all too difficult to control to draw any hard conclusions. However, added to the research that has gone before, our premise looks promising. (See Appendix 2 for a more detailed description of this project.)

5. Muscle patterns also can be (and often are) imitated unconsciously. During normal situations of interpersonal contact, it is common for people to mirror the facial and postural muscular patterns of another.

This is the area of research that is the most comprehensive. Numerous studies confirm that people unconsciously mirror each other all of the time. Morris (1979) called it a "postural echo," while Hatfield and colleagues (1992, 1994) called it "emotional contagion."

Hess and Blairy (2001) surreptitiously filmed the faces of subjects while they observed videos of people expressing various feelings. They found that the subjects consistently unconsciously mimicked the happy, angry, and sad expressions on the faces of the people in the videos. You may also have observed what Zajonc, Adelmann, Murphy, and Niedenthal (1987) confirmed: Many couples who stay together over many years grow to look like each other. The most logical explanation for this phenomenon is that couples tend to mimic each other's expression habitually, eventually leading to an actual observable, physical change. I have noticed that long-term couples often have the same mannerisms—how they use their hands or nod when they talk or listen—regardless of whether I am seeing them together or individually. Interestingly, I have even noted that able-bodied spouses can take on some of the mannerisms of handicapped partners, making them look somewhat disabled even though they are not.

Researchers have also observed that individuals in dyads mirror the other's movements during conversations (Hatfield et al., 1994; Kendon, 1970; LaFrance, 1976, 1979). This one you can easily confirm yourself. At your local café or favorite restaurant, or across the dinner table, observe pairs who are in close conversation and notice how often one copies the other's facial expression (e.g., smile, frown), gesture (e.g., drumming fingers, nodding), or postural element (e.g., resting head on hand, crossing legs). Remember also to pay attention to their feet, as foot tapping is often a shared behavior.

Can facial mirroring occur even when subjects have no idea they are being exposed to emotional facial expressions? In an intriguing study, subjects were shown a series of faces with neutral expressions interspersed with very quick flashes of faces with happy or angry expressions. The emotional faces were shown with such speed that it was not possible for the subjects to register seeing them consciously. Still, they mimicked the emotional facial expressions (Dimberg, 1982; Dimberg et al., 2000).

   6. Unconscious mirroring will also induce associated ANS reactions and feelings.

In the aforementioned study by Hess and Blairy (2001), it was also found that subjects noticed changes in their own moods that corresponded to the expression they were unconsciously mimicking.

Levenson and Ruef (1997) found that when one person copies another's facial expression, both the feeling and emotion (physical) responses are set in motion. They identified a direct link between facial expressions and feelings, smiles being particularly powerful for eliciting pleasant feelings.

In two simple experiments, Paccalin and Jeannerod (2000) demonstrated that sedentary spectators synchronize their breathing with the respiration of a performing athlete. Most people experienced muscle contractions in sympathy with the effort of others, for example while watching someone exert great effort to loosen the lid on a well sealed jar, or when watching downhill skiing on television.

It is also common to react to another's pain. Hodges and Wegner noted, "observing a person who touches a stove and winces causes us to wince, and, via physiological feedback from the set of muscles required to wince, I too can almost feel the burn" (1997, p. 316).

7. Instinctive synchrony of affective and ANS states in others may have an evolutionary role for survival of the species.

Because facial mimicry makes it possible to experience the emotional and feeling state of another, Levenson and associates (1990) saw it as more than a simple social signal. They believed that such behavior may serve as the basis for the creation of empathy, including attachment and bonding. In other studies, a clear connection between postural mimicry and rapport was found. As people copy one another's postures and movements, they get to know each other better and feel more positive about each other (Levenson & Ruef, 1997). When in danger, a whole group of people can synchronize their nervous systems to better respond to the danger.

The phenomenon of menstrual synchrony may have an evolutionary purpose (McClintock, 1971; Weller & Weller, 1993). Perhaps it served the needs of primitive clans for women to be fertile at the same time. Though I could not find scientific references, I have begun to wonder about the function of the highly contagious gag reflex. Perhaps it played a significant role in the survival of early hunter-gatherer tribes. Imagine a hungry group coming upon a new plant or a dead animal. They all begin to eat greedily. Then, one vomits and they all reflexively follow in turn. If the plant was poisoned or the animal diseased, lives may have been spared and the survival of the tribe aided.

8. Sometimes somatic empathy manifests as what seems to be mind reading, intuition, or ESP. However it can also have negative consequences for the unaware participant.

Internal feedback from mimicry (as described above) is the likely mechanism underlying emotional contagion. One person's emotion is "caught" by another, as facial or postural mirroring creates a similar internal experience (Hatfield et al., 1994). This hypothesis is supported by several studies which demonstrate that emotions can be created by mimicking muscle contractions associated with particular emotions (Adolphs, Damasio, Tranel, Cooper, & Damasio, 2000; Blairy, Herrera, & Hess, 1999; Duclos et al., 1989; Hess & Blairy, 2001). Further, in pilot studies Shiffrar and I documented preliminary evidence that more than emotion may be received via the action of mimicking another's posture (see Appendix 2). Many of our subjects intuited actual information, correctly guessing themes and actual situations in the memories of the models they were copying (Rothschild & Shiffrar, 2003, 2004).

A 1988 study by Miller, Stiff, and Ellis predicted the current wave of interest in compassion fatigue. They found that emotional contagion was a precursor to burnout among human service workers. The workers who were most easily infected by the feelings of those they were assisting were the most vulnerable to burnout.

9. The activity of the brain's mirror neurons may account for some portion of unconscious mimicry.

As early as 1995, Fadiga and colleagues were speculating about the existence of a visual-motor matching system. The discovery of mirror neurons confirmed their hunch. Such a system accounts for the common automatic reactions we all have when we observe actions in others. Yawning and laughter are the most familiar behaviors that people habitually copy.

Considered in their entirety, these nine points make a solid case that empathy is more than just a cognitive and emotional mechanism. Body processes are intimately involved.

Somatic empathy is expressed through the motor division of the nervous system (somatic nerves control the skeletal muscles, and autonomic nerves control the visceral muscles) and is perceived through the sensory nervous system: the five senses (exteroceptors) and balance, internal sensations, and proprioception (interoceptors).

The following is a rather extreme example of what body-to-body empathy may look like during a therapy session.

Gavin, a new child psychologist in private practice, particularly enjoyed using play therapy and the sand tray with his young patients. Observing one of his sessions through a one-way mirror was a fascinating experience. The interaction between Gavin and his patient was akin to watching a game of emotional follow-the-leader. When the child smiled, Gavin smiled. The child frowned; Gavin frowned. The patient raised her eyebrows, and Gavin's followed suit. No facial expression was initiated by the girl that was not mimicked by her therapist shortly thereafter. Gavin also mimicked his young client's breathing at times. Sighs appeared to be particularly contagious. Meeting with Gavin later that day, I asked him what the child had been feeling and what his own feelings had been during that hour. His oral report was congruent with what I had seen. He was catching the child's feelings. When I asked him how that might be possible, he had no clue. But when we looked at a video of the session together, he began to laugh. He saw it immediately: "My face is always an exact copy of hers!" Once I pointed it out, he could clearly see when he mimicked her breathing. By copying the girl's facial expression as well as breathing pattern, he tuned into and caught her feelings. It was unconscious; he was not trying to do it. He was truly surprised when he saw himself.

Of course, not all therapists mimic to the same degree that Gavin demonstrated. Some are especially self-aware and body aware and notice when they are and are not copying the client's expressions and breathing. Others may mimic purposefully to empathize with or to get a taste of the client's feelings. But plenty of practitioners, like Gavin, habitually and unconsciously copy client facial expressions, breathing patterns, and postures. Not only are they unconscious of the process, most important, they are clueless about the price their mimicry may be exacting from them.

The next sections build on the hypothesis of somatic empathy with additional illustrations of active postural and facial mirroring. Guidance in becoming more aware of somatic empathy between you and your clients is offered, including exercises for practice. It is hoped that by the end of this chapter, you will be better equipped to identify when your feelings, body sensations, and actions are the result of empathy with your client and when they are not. Subsequent chapters offer additional practical tools for putting you in charge of how—and how much—you empathize with your clients, giving you the choice.

Mirroring and Mimicry

Help me never to judge another until I have walked in his moccasins.

—*Native American Prayer*

As the saying goes, "Imitation is the most sincere form of flattery." It is also the quickest way to get a take on what another person is feeling. As discussed above, the human tendency to copy facial expressions, postures, and mannerisms is usually unconscious, though it is a common feature of interaction with others. Chartrand and Bargh (1999) called it *the chameleon effect*. In fact, it has been found that people with a high tendency for empathy will copy others more than those who test low for empathy (Lakin, Jefferis, Cheng, & Chartrand, 2003). Mimicry is the basis for many things we learn, including speech, table manners, and tying our shoes. You might even consider whether your therapeutic style has elements of mimicking a therapist you have admired or whether any of your colleagues resemble a mentor. The exact styles of well-known clinicians have often (and sometimes unfortunately) been copied; examples include Sigmund Freud in the 1950s and Fredrik Perls and Carl Rogers in the 1960s and 1970s.

Though facial and postural mimicry are usually automatic, by increasing your self-awareness and body awareness you can observe for yourself how much you imitate those around you and how often they imitate you. The next time you see a client, have lunch with a friend, or talk with your spouse, check how often aspects of your posture have become the same as theirs. Also try leaning your hand on your head or crossing your legs. Then see how long it takes for the other person to do the same. You can become a scientist, testing imitative behavior in your own professional and social circles.

THE ROOTS OF THE HYPOTHESIS

In the late 1960s, one of my closest friends, Nancy Curtis, was studying to be a physical therapist. Sometimes, while walking down the street, she would notice a stranger walking in a manner she considered interesting. Unabashedly, she would proceed to mimic the gait of that stranger as I followed behind. She would then tell me what she felt in her body, where that person might have an injury, or some such. At first I was embarrassed by her behavior and worried about what would happen if she was caught, that is, detected by her subject. I did not want her to shame anyone. Nancy insisted she knew what she was doing and no one would get hurt. She was careful, she reassured me, only to mimic at a discreet distance; her subjects never saw what she was doing, never noticed. After witnessing her actions several times, I became reassured that she never exaggerated her mimicry; it never became mockery. She was subtle enough that anyone looking at her would, if they even noticed, just think she had the different gait herself. I was more aware of it because she told me what she was doing.

This strange behavior was Nancy's way of practicing gait diagnosis (analyzing how someone walked), a critically important tool for a physical therapist. She found that she could make the most accurate evaluation if she could feel in her own body what was going on in the hip, ankle, or foot of her subject (and later, her patients). As a novice, for her, mere visual observation was not enough.

I became fascinated by the practice and asked Nancy to teach me how to do it. Actually, it was quite easy and I caught on quickly. I learned to copy (mimic) the gaits of people walking in front of me. At first, gait mimicry was a game for me, just an interesting way to find out what was going on in someone's body. It also stirred some fascinating conversations about body mechanics with Nancy. I became pretty good at it, and my "diagnosis" was often in agreement with hers.

A few years later as I began to study psychotherapy and body psychotherapy, I became more self-aware as I practiced various training exercises. The result piqued my interest in body mimicry even more. I realized that copying people's gaits changed more than just my way of walking. Sometimes a different emotion stirred in me and I would find myself suddenly in a different mood. For example, following behind a youth with a confident stride, I might feel a little cocky myself. On some occasions, visual images and thoughts emerged that I could not account for. I began to wonder: By copying another's manner of walking, was I actually getting a little peek into what it was like to be him? When I copied a gait, was I walking in her moccasins, so to speak?

As discussed in the previous section, it is well documented that observation of another's movement alone can influence the behavior of the observer. Chartrand and Bargh (1999) showed that experimental subjects sitting with a research associate, who was cued to scratch his nose, tended to follow suit. The same effect resulted when the associate shook his foot. Imitation is innate. Infants as young as 42 minutes old have been seen to mimic the facial expression of a parent (Meltzoff & Moore, 1983, 1989).

Even more crucial, observing another's movement can also influence emotions and more complex behavior. In their classic studies, Bandura, Ross, and Ross (1963) demonstrated that having children watch a film with aggressive behavior increased their levels of aggression through imitation. Just the experience of adopting an emotion-associated posture can stimulate a change in emotional experience (Duclos et al., 1989). All told, it is undeniable, as Niedenthal, Barsalou, Winkielman, Krauth-Gruber, and Ric (in press) concluded: The body is an integral repository for social and emotional information processing.

What more might be happening when people imitate each other's behavior and expressions? Based on the study by Bandura and colleagues and the like, we know feelings are communicated through imitated actions. Hess and Blairy (2001) found that happiness and sadness were exchanged when a subject observed and then mimicked a facial expression. On these bases, it becomes reasonable to wonder just what information might be exchanged between two people when each emulates the other's behavior, posture, or facial expression. Perhaps you already have an idea; you may have experienced something similar yourself. Have you ever known by your own sensations or feelings how your client, child, friend, or spouse was feeling before they told you? Have you ever seen in your mind's eye what your client later described? The next section further clarifies at least one of the mechanisms at work in these phenomena.

POSTURAL MIRRORING

Postural mirroring is the term that has been coined for the mimicry of another's physical posture, including facial expressions, and the communication of emotional and other information that often accompanies such behavior. It appears the term was used first by dance therapists. They have long utilized postural mirroring as a common tool of their trade. A dance therapist will use mirroring to get a feel for her clients, and also to give feedback on what is observed and felt (Siegel, 1984). When a client stands or moves in a certain way, the dance therapist will follow suit. The practice was likely inspired by Wilhelm Reich, the father of body psychotherapy. In his classic, *Character Analysis*, he wrote, "The patient's expressive movements involuntarily bring about *an imitation* in our own organism. By [actively] imitating these movements, we 'sense' and understand the expression in ourselves and, consequently, in the patient" (Reich, 1972, p. 362).

Postural mirroring involves mimicry—whether conscious or unconscious. Sometimes we do it on purpose. Anytime we copy a posture, an expression, or the breathing pattern of another person, we are using postural mirroring.

As children, we mimicked our parents, teachers, and older siblings in order to learn many tasks: holding a pencil, playing hopscotch, and so on. Anytime a parent, teacher, or sibling said, "Watch and then do it like me," we were being encouraged to mimic. We also mimicked others as we learned how to behave in different milieus: at the table, at school, on the playground, and so forth. (When living in Denmark, I was often—sometimes too often—admonished to mimic those around me rather than "behaving like a typical American.") Sometimes children take their mimicry a step further toward actual postural mirroring when they try to take on the mannerisms or speech of a parent, friend, actor, or pop star they admire, trying to act and be just like them.

Next time you are at a park or a shopping center, take a look at pairs of parents and children. How does the child sit, stand, or walk like the parent? Posture depends somewhat on build, but it is also habituated through mimicry. Some families walk erect, some slump. Not only does bone structure determine a common family posture, but mimicry also plays a role. Notice your own children at the dinner table. Whom do they sit like? Whom do their manners remind you of: their friends, you, your spouse? Manners are also learned through mimicry.

Consider for a minute or two how you sit or stand in relationship to the individuals you help—you might want to pay attention in one or two sessions to get an idea. Start to notice when you assume their same posture, wholly or partially. Do you have a tendency to cross your legs, sit on the edge of your seat, slump, or breathe like your client? Do you copy their expression onto your own face in an attempt to communicate that you understand what they are feeling—smiling, lowering your eyebrows, clenching your teeth? Have you ever slowed your breathing in the hope that your panicking client would follow suit, calming his own panicked gasps? If you answer yes to any of these questions, then you already know (or are learning) something about mirroring. Continuing to pay attention to your own posture and expressions when you are with your clients will further increase your awareness of how much you do or do not mirror. In a few pages, I will begin to look at how you might use that awareness to better care for yourself during and following therapy sessions.

POSTURAL MIRRORING AND EMPATHY

As mentioned previously, empathy has to do with feeling what another is feeling. Since mirroring appears to enhance that likelihood, it just may be a major mechanism of empathy. You can try this yourself with a client, friend, or family member: Consciously mimic his respiration pattern, posture, or facial expression. Then guess what he is feeling and ask if you are correct. You can also try this more structured exercise with a friend or colleague:

1. Both of you stand up and each take stock of your own physical and emotional state. What sensations are you aware of (temperature, aches and pains, tension/relaxation, etc.)? What are you feeling emotionally?
2. Follow, literally, in the other person's footsteps. Have her walk normally in front of you. To the best of your

ability, copy her posture and gait. Do this for a minute or so.

3. Notice what you have to do with your own body to walk like her. How are you using your muscles and balance differently? Be as specific as possible.

4. Take stock of what you are feeling emotionally. Is it the same or different than before you walked like her?

5. Compare with each other what you were sensing in your bodies and feeling in your emotions while walking in this way. It will not happen every time, but you may find quite a bit of correspondence in what each of you were sensing and feeling.

This exercise demonstrates the essence of postural mirroring: Mimicking another's posture or movement which usually results in empathizing with his physical and emotional state. *It is that simple.* Actors have been doing this for centuries, often using postural mirroring to become the person they are to play on screen or stage. Some actors will spend many hours observing, in person or on film, an individual they are to portray, consciously mimicking posture, mannerisms, and speech. One of the most successful of these was Jamie Foxx in his portrayal of Ray Charles in *Ray*, for which he won a best actor Oscar in 2005. Some viewers said they could not distinguish the two.

Feeling What the Other Feels

I have informally conducted the above exercise and a more formal mirroring exercise (see the section, Conscious Postural Mirroring) with hundreds of psychotherapists and body psychotherapists. Predictably, physical experiences are consistently parallel because the exercises involve the mimicking of posture and movement. Also predictably, based on the research reviewed in previous sections, there is also consistent emotional resonance—partners experiencing the same feelings. What accounts for this? Do physical movement and posture also communicate somato-emotional states that underpin feeling? Experiments on posture mimicry by Duclos and colleagues (1989) support this premise. They do not, however, explain the mechanism. We need to look further.

Antonio Damasio's (1994) concept of somatic markers may account for at least some of this phenomenon. To review his theory, Damasio posited that the experience of emotions is composed of body sensations that are elicited in response to various stimuli. Those sensations, and their related emotions, become encoded and then stored as implicit memories associated with the stimuli that originally evoked them (possibly similar to classical conditioning). Remember: Damasio clarified a distinction between emotion and feeling. The former includes all things physical: sensations, facial expressions, muscle contractions, autonomic fluctuations, and so on. When the aggregate of that body information reaches the frontal cortex, a label is then applied—angry, scared, sad, happy, or some such—which is what he called "feeling."

Following Damasio's theory, it becomes logical that feelings could be communicated through mirroring. For example, when I mimic the posture and expression of my sad client, I am mimicking much of what comprises his emotion (for example, furrowing my brow, dropping the sides of my mouth, lowering my head, depressing my chest, etc.). As noted previously, adopting expressions and postures associated with emotions can stir the same familiar internal sensations (ache in the gut, fullness in the throat, even tears, etc.). My own frontal cortex assesses the information from my body and applies the label *sad*. That is one way (if not a major way) that I could "know" what my client is feeling at any one time. There are quotation marks around the word *know* because it is possible to misjudge. I would rarely (if ever) want to tell a client, "I know what you are feeling" before he had told me—both because I could be wrong and because I prefer not to lead a client in that way. Nonetheless, the information can be useful at times.

I can take this a step further, though, because an additional phenomenon is common when one mirrors another. Often (though not as consistently as with physical and emotional correspondence) a strong correlation of imagery, thoughts, and actual knowledge is communicated between two people. Sometimes we call it intuition or ESP.

MIRRORING RESEARCH

During a pilot study conducted in 2003 (Rothschild & Shiffrar, 2003, 2004) as part of a training course in Europe, I asked one of the group sponsors to silently model his posture after something reminiscent of an emotional situation from his life and to hold it steady for a few minutes. He struck a pose with one arm elevated behind him, the other reaching outward and down in front of him; his feet were about a foot and a half apart, placed one in front of the other; his torso bent slightly forward.

No words or verbal information of any kind were communicated to the group members. Half of the group was instructed to copy his posture, the other half just to observe it. Following the exercise, the group members filled out questionnaires indicating the physical sensations, feelings, thoughts, and images they experienced, and to guess what the model may have been remembering. After the group members had a chance to note their personal responses and fill out their questionnaires, the sponsor was allowed to speak. He told us that he had remembered being a teenager, saving a younger sibling from drowning in a stream in the woods.

The responses to the questionnaires from the mirroring half of the group were fascinating. No one had known what the situation was—none had somatic markers for anything similar. However, several in that half felt a powerful effort or struggle in their own bodies and a sense of urgency. Generally they reported feeling strong and focused. Fear was the predominant affect. Some had visual images of being outdoors and of water or trees.

Considering that the remembered scenario was something totally outside of the average person's experience, the results were quite astonishing. With the same group, another sponsor had modeled a posture in memory of something that would be quite familiar to almost anyone (i.e., most would have somatic markers for it); feeding her infant grandchild. The results were intriguing. Among both the mirroring and the observing halves, there was an extremely high correlation of sensations, emotions, and images (the mirroring group having the highest). In addition, the majority easily guessed that the situation had something to do with caring for a young child. Likely, these higher correlations could be predicted since just about every adult has somatic markers for caring for a baby. The results from these pilot experiments are compelling enough to warrant further study (see Appendix 2 for a more detailed description of this and similar projects.)

USING CONSCIOUS POSTURAL MIRRORING TO GAIN INFORMATION

Though the aim of this book is to reduce risks to therapist well-being, it is important to further discuss the use of conscious postural mirroring as an aid to the therapeutic process. The following case (Rothschild, 2004b) illustrates this.

When you want to get a literal feel for what it's like to be in your client's skin, you can consciously mirror some aspect of his or her behavior or expression. I tried this when I worked with Fred, a new college graduate who had come into therapy to address his anxiety about dealing with au-

thority on his first professional job. Though he'd grown up with a violent father who had beaten him regularly as a child, Fred couldn't see or feel any relationship between his childhood trauma and his current fear of standing up to his boss.

One afternoon, Fred arrived for his session deeply depressed. He'd been thinking about suicide, he said, but had no idea why. Admittedly, I wasn't sure either. To explore what might be going on, I asked him to describe what "suicidal" felt like in his body. To see if it could help my understanding, as I listened to his somatic report I tuned in by copying his flat facial expression and slumped posture. Almost immediately, I began to experience in my own body the sense of deadness Fred had just described to me. It reminded me of the freeze response that is an instinctive reaction to inescapable threat. All at once, a lightbulb flashed in my mind. "Fred," I asked, "have you ever seen a mouse that's been caught by a cat?" He nodded. "What does the mouse do?" I prodded. "It plays dead," he replied, his face beginning to brighten with interest. We then discussed the protective function of freezing for all prey, both animals and people. Finally, I asked Fred if he'd ever reacted that way himself.

"Yeah," he said softly, "when my dad beat me." As his father hit him, he told me, his body would lose all power and "go dead." For the first time, he made a felt connection between his childhood horrors and his current emotional state. It seemed a lightbulb had also come on in Fred's mind. As he began to talk thoughtfully about his own "internal mouse," his body posture gradually became more upright and animated, and by the end of the session he reported that his thoughts of suicide had receded.

Could I have helped Fred make this breakthrough with talk alone? Perhaps, but it would likely have entailed several more sessions full of the usual conversational roundabouts, byways, and detours. Instead, by mirroring him, I was able to quickly feel and then understand Fred's deadness.

As can be seen, this is a useful therapeutic tool. However, there is an important caveat: While purposefully synchronizing with your client can often provide added insight or even jump-start a stalled session, be aware that the data you pick up are not infallible. Just as gaps can occur between speaker and listener in verbal communication, so can somatic communication be distorted by your own filters. If, for example, you mimic your client's head tilt and get a feeling of anxiety in your chest, your client may indeed be anxious. But it also could be that you habitually tilt your head in that way when *you* are anxious, so that mirroring that posture triggers a different emotion in you. So, as I did with Fred, be sure to check out your bodily hunches with your clients and not jump to conclusions.

THE RISKS OF UNCONSCIOUS POSTURAL MIRRORING

I learned about some of the risks of postural mirroring the hard way, through discomforting and distressing personal experiences with my clients. While there were several difficult incidents, one in particular stands out (Rothschild, 2004b).

I had been seeing Ronald for about a year when, one day, he came to his session absolutely furious with me. He was so angry he could neither face me nor speak. He had scheduled a double session and during the first hour he sat turned away from me with his head bowed, the rest of his body very tense and slightly shaking. I tried to make contact with him using my usual supply of therapeutic phrases: "You seem very angry." "It must be very difficult for you." And so forth. He wouldn't have any of it. Each effort at contact and empathy seemed to depart my lips, float out into the room a foot or so, and then fall flat on the floor with a thump. Finally, I told myself to keep quiet, let him be in his anger, and wait for him to contact me. It seemed as though it was going to take a while and, frankly, I began to get a little bored. Thinking about things I had learned during my training years, I decided to mimic his posture, just to see if I could gain any insight into what was going on with him. Up until that time, I had used such techniques to facilitate getting a sense of the client. I wasn't prepared for the physical and emotional impact it would later have on me.

Shortly after I copied Ronald's posture, he began to speak to me and tell me how angry he was. Could he have sensed my mimicry even though he wasn't looking? Was it possible that my nonverbal empathetic posture communicated something to him more potent than words? Or was the timing coincidental? Actually, I don't know. But what Ronald perceived is not pertinent here. Most important is that I forgot: I had first mirrored him consciously, and I unconsciously continued as I became absorbed in his words and emotional expression. We went on with the session, resolving some (but not all) of his anger. He felt better when he left.

When he closed the door and I had only myself to focus on, I found I did NOT *feel better. In fact, I was in a rage. I was furious. It was very uncomfortable and I became very distressed. I tried to work it out by yelling, stomping, and hitting a pillow, but it wouldn't abate. I tried to figure out why I was so angry. Was I angry with Ronald? Something in my life? Something from my past? I could not figure it out. My upset went on for several hours, barely containable as I saw other clients.*

Finally, when I was free in the afternoon, I called a close friend and colleague. I had to tell someone how upset and confused I was. My friend grasped the situation immediately. She asked me, "When did it start? What were you doing?" When I recounted the session with Ronald, she simply said, "Oh, Babette! You were mirroring him." As soon as she said it, I remembered what I had begun doing consciously and then had forgotten. I immediately felt better. It was as though she had thrown warm water on me;

the anger just melted off. That feeling of anger did not belong to me—I had adopted it from Ronald!

I learned an important lesson that day: Never take postural mirroring for granted. Always pay attention to reversing it during sessions, or at the least, immediately after a client leaves. Never forget its power.

Mirroring Versus Projective Identification

To some therapists, what happened between Ronald and me may look like a textbook case of projective identification—a case of Ronald "putting" his uncomfortable feelings into me and thereby "inducing" my fury. I could not disagree more. I was a full participant in the process: Only after I actively mirrored Ronald did I begin to feel angry. But while my mimicry was entirely conscious—if later forgotten—I believe that this kind of brain-to-brain/body-to-body communication occurs at an unconscious level between clients and therapists all the time. The next time you feel that you may be suffering from the impact of a projective identification, you may need to look no further than your own body to discover whether you have mimicked your client's posture, facial expression, or breathing pattern. Routinely adding such a simple step could eliminate blaming clients for feelings that are, in fact, rooted in your own naturally responsive neural circuitry.

There is liberation here, particularly for therapists who often find themselves on the edge of emotional overload. Active awareness of your own neurally mediated role in absorbing clients' feelings can help you to control the contagion. Once you become aware of your mimicry, any behavior that brings you back to the sensations and feelings of your own body— and out of synchronization with the client—will help you to apply the "empathy brakes." You might stretch, take a drink of water, get up to fetch a pen, or write some notes. These steps will not short-circuit access to all dimensions of empathy, but rather will allow you to return to yourself, to a place of clarity, presence, and helpful attunement to your client.

Making Unconscious Mirroring Conscious

By now, many readers may have realized that postural mirroring is something they do with clients habitually and unconsciously. You might even be beginning to wonder if some of the feelings you have during and following client sessions have something to do with postural mirroring. If so, then a discussion of how to help you make that unconscious process conscious could be useful at this point. That is the first step toward the skill of choosing when to mirror and when not to mirror.

Basically, mindfulness (being aware) is all that is needed for you to pay attention to yourself. At least from time to time during encounters with your clients (or, for that matter, meetings with your colleagues and time spent with family and friends), take a few seconds to take stock. In the sections Facial and Postural Awareness, Conscious Postural Mirroring, Unmirroring, and Strengthening the Observer, techniques and strategies for increasing body and self-awareness are described in detail.

WHEN A CLIENT FEELS YOUR PAIN

Empathy, of course, is a two-way street. Our clients often unconsciously adopt our body patterns and take on our corresponding emotional states. Many therapists instinctively foster this process. When, for example, you slow your own breathing and your anxious client subsequently slows his, you are likely engaging his mirror neurons. No words need be exchanged for the client to gradually match your slower respiration and begin to calm down. But beware: If a clinician's calm state is contagious, so too is his agitation. When a client is unusually out of sorts on a day when you have not been in a good mood, you might consider if your client is tuning in to *you*. Clients can pick up all sorts of feelings and states from the therapist. Here is a lighter example.

> *One morning, upon returning to Copenhagen (my then home) after a long visit to the United States, I was suffering from a particularly nasty case of jet lag. Though exhausted and headachy, I jumped right into my usual work schedule. At the end of my afternoon session with Helle, I asked her, per usual, "How are you feeling?" Helle proceeded to describe my jet lag in precise detail. "I feel very tired, and there's a feeling of pressure in my forehead," she said, rubbing her eyebrows. "I also feel an odd heaviness in my chest. And I'm hungry, though I shouldn't be. I ate a good lunch just before I came."*
>
> *I suggested to Helle that she stand up and walk around the room, hoping that the physical activity would move her out of my somatic sphere of influence and back into contact with her own body. After pacing for a minute or two, she returned to her chair, noticeably more energetic. "My exhaustion and hunger have disappeared!" she reported. I then told her how I was feeling, that she had described my sensations precisely.*
>
> *Since consciousness is an important part of the process of controlling the neuronal dance, we spent a few minutes tracking down how Helle had caught my state. In retracing her steps—and postures—she realized she had rested her head on her hand as I had tiredly done. That ordinary act of unconscious mimicry was enough to make her vulnerable to feeling my jet lag and the other-time-zone hunger that accompanied it.*

As mentioned earlier, conscious mimicry can be used to facilitate a greater knowledge and rapport with your client. But whether it happens consciously or unconsciously, mimicry and the perception of mimicry are "a kind of natural 'social glue' that produces empathic understanding and even greater [support] between people, without their having to intend or try to have this happen" (Chartrand & Bargh, 1999, p. 897).

SKILL BUILDING

Facial and Postural Awareness

[T]he sight of a face that is happy, loving, angry, sad, or fearful can cause the viewer to mimic elements of that face and, consequently, to catch the other's emotions.

—Hatfield and colleagues (1994, p. 53)

Humans routinely mimic the facial expressions of others. This is readily observable in public places and at gatherings of family or friends. You will find that the expressions on the faces of people in pairs or small groups often match. Facial mimicry is a reflex that usually happens outside our awareness. But even when we are paying attention, it can sometimes be difficult to stop it. As you walk down the street or through a store, for example, how often do you reflexively smile in response to the smile of a stranger? Probably often, perhaps even more often than you know. Have you ever tried to not smile back? My own experimental attempts have been very difficult and required a good deal of effort. But it does get easier with practice.

In the therapy room, psychotherapists will sometimes consciously alter their facial expression to express empathy to a client, a nonverbal message: "I understand what you are feeling (or going through)." Usually the effect is temporary, but sometimes it can be long-lasting and can deeply affect the therapist, particularly when copying the client's facial expression is not conscious.

Marlene was a clinical social worker in a shelter for battered women. She had grown up in a relatively cohesive family and believed she had many resources for her difficult job. Generally, she was emotionally and physically healthy, taking regular vacations, working out, eating well, and making use of her very supportive network.

Though Marlene had not had the same kinds of life experiences as the women she was helping, she felt she was

able to relate deeply. She genuinely cared about the resi-
dents of the shelter, crying and laughing with them, wor-
rying for their safety when they were discharged, cele-
brating their triumphs, and grieving for those who met
tragedy.

As much as she loved her work, after three years at the
shelter, Marlene began to feel she was burning out. She
found it increasingly difficult to get up and go to work.
Sometimes, when she was by herself, she found herself
crying about the hopelessness of life. She had never
thought of herself as prone to depression before, but she
was considering asking her doctor for antidepressant med-
ication.

What happened to Marlene? Nothing in her past linked
her to the experiences of these women, yet her level of empathy was so great that her ability to work was becoming
compromised. The key here may lie in the depth of her empathy, likely deeper than she ever realized.

FACIAL FEEDBACK HYPOTHESIS

[F]acial mimicry is arguably the expressive behavior most closely
tied to emotional processes in general and to emotional rapport
and knowledge in particular . . . both theory and data suggest
that the synchrony of interactants' facial expressions can lead
fairly directly to the commonality of emotional states across
individuals.

—*Levenson and Ruef* (1997, p. 56)

Adopting a particular facial expression will communicate
emotional information to the brain. The same process is involved whether the facial expression is generated inside you
or is set in motion by copying the expression of another. The
facial feedback hypothesis was first proposed by Silvan
Tompkins (1963). He found that the position or pattern of
facial muscles leads to subjective feelings of emotion, so that
mimicking an emotion will activate the same emotion. For

example, turning down the sides of the mouth will generate an internal feeling of sadness. Actors use the principles of this hypothesis to produce the emotions they portray.

Paul Ekman agreed that altering facial expression can actually cause emotion. He found that induced facial expression changes physiological responses throughout the body, specifically in the autonomic nervous system, affecting such factors as heart rate and skin temperature. Each facial expression produces a different pattern. For example, anger raises heartbeat and skin temperature; disgust lowers them (Ekman et al., 1983). Recalling the earlier discussion on the sensory nervous system and Damasio's somatic marker theory, the facial feedback hypothesis makes more sense. The change in muscular position activates interoceptive nerves, which are linked to somatic markers and give feedback to the brain on the experience of emotion.

In a corroborating study by Ulf Dimberg (1982), college students showed increased activity in their cheek muscles while viewing happy, smiling faces and increased activity in their brow muscles when viewing angry, scowling faces. Dimberg also found that ANS activity in the students was altered per Ekman's findings. It is relevant for practitioners that Dimberg observed that ANS reactions to happy faces were short-lived, while reactions to angry faces were longer lasting. Maybe that is a partial explanation for why my reaction to Ronald (see p. 69) persisted over so many hours.

Back to Marlene—In a consultation session, she talked about her work and her growing burnout. The more she talked, I noticed, the more she adopted the facial expression of someone who has lived through terrible trauma. She really began to look beaten down. As this was not actually the case for her, I became curious about how she related to her clients. "How much of the time," I asked, "do you feel your client's experience?" "Most of the time, I think," she replied. "In social work school I was taught that empathy was my primary tool for connecting to my clients." I asked if she knew how she accomplished such a resonance. She wasn't sure, so I suggested that in the next week she pay greater attention to her body and her face when working with clients.

At the next consultation, Marlene was eager to tell me that she had paid a lot of attention. She often noticed her face adopting expressions similar to those of her clients, or at least it felt that way from the inside. She could feel her jaw clench and her eyes harden when a client was expressing anger, and she recognized a softness around her eyes and a catch in her throat when one cried.

Next, as an experiment, I asked her to remember a particular client's expression, adopt it on her own face as she felt it, and then look in the mirror to see if that was correct. When she looked, she was surprised to see just how much she looked like that client. "I didn't know I could be so accurate!" she exclaimed. "And what do you feel emotionally when you adopt that expression?" I asked. She answered rather quickly, "Anxious and depressed." I probed further, "Does that have any correlation to that client's feelings?" Marlene nodded slowly. I could almost see the lightbulb turning on over her head. "Do you think this has something to do with why I am feeling so depressed?"

Yes, I did. Marlene and I spent much of the consultation going over facial feedback theory. I then suggested that during the following week she experiment with the same client, sometimes consciously adopting a different facial expression. We discussed what kinds of expressions she might adopt that would convey understanding and empathy, without being a copy of the client's expression. In addition, I wanted her to notice how she felt, herself, before and after each session.

At our next meeting, Marlene was enthusiastic. Consciously changing her facial expression, while difficult, had definitely had an emotional impact. She had felt in a better mood following the session with her target client than she did with other clients that week. She decided that she wanted to take the experiment further and try paying attention to and altering her facial expression with more clients. Over the next few months, Marlene found that her *depression lifted significantly. She was still distressed by the severity of trauma her clients had to deal with, but her own day-to-day functioning had improved significantly.*

CONTROLLING FACIAL MIMICRY

The exercises below will help you to increase awareness of, and control over, your own propensity for facial mirroring.

Observing and Controlling the Smiling Reflex

1. On your next trip to the grocery store, see how many people you can catch smiling in response to your smiling at them. As you walk down the aisles and check out, purposely smile and notice how people respond.
2. During an average day or outing, count how often you smile in response to a smile from another.
3. Then, on several more outings, practice not smiling reflexively in response to some stranger's smile. You may find this harder than you would think, so do not be discouraged if it takes you several tries to get the hang of it.

Controlling Facial Mimicry of Athletes and Film Actors

1. Either watching television or at the movies, pay attention to your facial expression when an athlete or actor is expressing a strong emotion.
2. Identify which expressions are the most habitual for you to copy.
3. Practice not copying those expressions during subsequent television programs or films.

APPLICATIONS WITH YOUR CLIENTS: AWARENESS OF FACIAL MIRRORING

Videotaping one or more therapy sessions with at least one client is an ideal way to gain awareness of your propensity to mirror client facial expressions. The camera should be angled to take in both of you. The steps below can be used instead of or in addition to videotaping.

Pre-session Inventory

1. Start with one client whose feelings you seem vulnerable to or one who tends to hang around in your feelings or thoughts after sessions.

2. Immediately prior to the next session with that client, take an inventory of how you are feeling emotionally. Include what your facial expression feels like from the inside. It will probably be helpful to write this down so you remember exactly.

3. Before you go to meet your client, look in a mirror and see what your facial expression actually looks like pre-session. Include the muscles around your forehead, mouth, cheeks, and eyes, and the expression of your eyes. Jot all of this down.

4. Include in your session notes—several times during the session—the client's feelings and facial expression.

5. At least twice (even better, three or four times) take a quick inventory of your own feelings and what your facial expression feels like. Make a note.

6. Also during the session, write down when you notice your facial expression changing, and check to see if the client's expression has also changed.

Post-session Evaluation

1. Immediately following the session, make note of your postsession feelings, indicating if any are similar to the feelings your client was expressing or suppressing during the session.

2. Next, look in the mirror to see what your facial expression looks like. How is it different than before the session? Is it reflective of your own mood or your client's?

Post-session Intervention

1. If your facial expression is a mirror of your client's, move your facial muscles around, making faces at yourself. Notice if or how that changes your mood.
2. Think of something or someone pleasant and notice if or how that changes your facial expression.

In-session Intervention

1. At the next session with this same client, consciously change your facial expression to something different than your client's three times during the hour. Of course you will not want to smile if your client is feeling upset, or make an angry face at a skittish client. But you can adopt a neutral expression, neither happy nor upset (you may need to practice this with a mirror before the session). Notice your mood during the session and when your client has left. Is it the same or different than you usually feel after seeing this client?
2. If you find it difficult to change your expression when you are with your client, practice first in other encounters: friends, family, and so on. You could also role-play with a colleague.
3. When you are successful in controlling your facial expressions with one client, move on to another and start again at the beginning of the exercise above.
4. Do not forget that you can always adopt the same expression as your client when you feel that is of benefit to the client and poses little or no risk to your own well-being. Learning to control automatic facial mirroring gives you more choices: to mirror or not to mirror, depending on what is most useful for the therapy and what benefits the well-being of both you and your client.

It is easy to assume that clients want us to feel along with them, and some surely do. However, many clients much prefer

for the therapist—and others—to stay out of emotional resonance (to stay in your own chair, as I discuss in Chapter 5). I
remember a particular group therapy session when a young
woman arrived in tears, reporting the breakup of her marriage.
As she sobbed her story, the other group members were deeply
touched, many crying along with her. At the end of the session, the woman thanked everyone for the support. She also
reported that she appreciated the empathy of the group but
found that she kept her eyes riveted on me—the one person
there who was not distressed with her. She felt she needed to
anchor herself with someone who was "solid and unmoved." I
asked if she had felt me to be indifferent. "Oh, no," she replied.
"I know you care, but I was relieved you didn't look upset like
everyone else. Their feelings were validating, but I'm going to
need stability to get my footing back."

Conscious Postural Mirroring

> When I wish to find out how wise, or how stupid, or how good, or
> how wicked is anyone, or what are his thoughts at the moment, I
> fashion the expression of my face, as accurately as possible, in
> accordance with the expression of his, and then wait to see what
> thoughts or sentiments arise in my mind or heart, as if to match or
> correspond with the expression.
> —*School boy in Poe's* The Purloined Letter (1984)

As has been discussed, in addition to facial mirroring, humans frequently and habitually copy the postures of others.
This can also be readily observed in public places: couples
both resting their heads on hands, legs crossed in the same
way, looking down or away at the same time, simultaneous
stretching, leg rocking, finger drumming, and so forth. Also
notice groups of teenagers, how they stand and slump alike.
    Postural mimicry follows a route similar to the facial
feedback hypothesis. That is, copying postures can also
trigger somatic mechanisms that give emotional feedback
to the brain. When I sit like you sit, I can experience what

you are feeling. Unconscious postural mirroring can wreak the same havoc as unconscious facial mirroring. However, when brought into awareness and used consciously and purposely, postural mirroring can be a powerful route to increased empathy.

Conscious mirroring is used in almost every body psychotherapy program (and some psychotherapy programs) to facilitate the therapist's capacity for insight into the client's situation and emotional state. As mentioned previously, the idea originated in dance therapy (Siegel, 1984). When conscious, time limited, and undertaken (and interrupted) with full awareness, it can be an extremely useful way to gain insight and enhance understanding in a psychotherapy setting.

The following exercise serves several purposes. First, it demonstrates what postural mirroring is and how to do it consciously. Second, it provides guidelines so you can practice it yourself if you so choose. Third, it will increase your awareness of any postural mirroring you might already be doing unconsciously.

MIRRORING EXERCISE

This exercise is intended to be done with a colleague who can discuss the results. Eventually, you may want to experiment with conscious mirroring with one or more of your clients, but this structured exercise is not advisable for that. This exercise can be used privately, with just one colleague, or as part of a group training or consultation session.

- In pairs, designate one as A and the other as B.
- From this point on, do not talk. At the end of the ex-

* *Caution:* Please take care with your choice of memory. Even when I have used this in training programs and have been very careful to repeatedly specify that the emotion should be low-key, therapists still choose car accidents, hospital emergency incidents, and the like. As a result of those kinds of choices, both partners have often ended up very upset. This really is a powerful exercise.

ercise, an instruction is given for discussion and comparing notes.

- Prior to starting, both partners should check their self-awareness to get a baseline to compare with. Notice any particulars in your body: temperature, muscle tension, breathing pattern, internal sensations, and so on. Also assess what you are feeling emotionally and your mood in general.
- First, A thinks of a situation with some emotional charge. It can be a pleasant or mildly unpleasant emotion (happy, sad, irritated, anxious, lust, etc.), so long as it is not traumatic or highly stressful. Keeping the emotional material low-key will make it easier to focus on the nuts and bolts of the skill building without being distracted by upsetting material.*
- Next, A takes a physical posture (sitting, standing, or crouching) that has something to do with that situation and maintains it. For example, if the situation has to do with driving a car, A might sit in a chair with raised arms feigning holding a steering wheel.
- While A maintains the position, B mirrors (copies) A's posture, getting into the exact same position as A.
- Then B takes note of the following:
  1. What do I have to do with my body to assume this posture? Which muscles do I tense, relax? Where do I twist, turn, bend? Do I bend or tip in any way?
  2. What sensations do I become aware of? What is my body temperature and how is it distributed? Is there tingling, numbness, pain, pleasure? Where?
  3. Do any images come to mind? What are the pictures, sounds, tastes, smells that emerge?
  4. What am I feeling emotionally? (happy, scared, sad, etc.)
  5. What thoughts (or other verbalizations, e.g., songs) are running through my head?
- Once B has checked points 1 through 5, B silently

guesses what kind of situation A is remembering. Then, B signals A that they both can relax the postures and sit down facing each other.

- Then B gives A a specific report. At this point A only listens and does not talk yet.
- B uses this structure for the feedback: "When I was standing/sitting/crouching like you . . .
    1. "I did . . . with my body [describe what B had to do to assume A's posture]."
    2. "I sensed in my body . . . [describe physical sensations]."
    3. "I saw/heard/smelled/tasted . . . [describe images]."
    4. "I felt . . . [emotion]."
    5. "I thought . . ."
    6. Lastly, B tells his guess.
- When B is finished, then it is A's turn to speak.
- A shares with B the situation that A was remembering, including what was happening in A's body, sensations, emotions, images, and thoughts.
- A and B discuss the similarities and differences in their experiences.

When giving feedback, remember to talk about your own experience. You may be accessing information about the other person, but what you are picking up is going through your own filters. There may or may not be correspondence. Information gained in this manner will likely provide you with some hunches about the other person's experience, but not knowledge until you have checked your accuracy. This is an important distinction: Sometimes therapists confuse intuition with fact, which can cause difficulties for the client. Always check out your hunches and take the other's word for whether or not you are on target.

Based on your discussion with your partner, take note of which elements you were most accurate with. Are you more sensitive to body sensations, emotions, visual images, auditory images, or thoughts? You may need to try this exercise several times, possibly with several people, before you reach a conclusion. Once you know your area of strength, you can maximize it by focusing on that element when you want to tune in. It will also tell you which element is your vulnerability if you are picking up too much (which is addressed in the section Unmirroring).

APPLICATIONS OF POSTURAL MIRRORING IN PSYCHOTHERAPY

Once you have grasped the tools of conscious mirroring, you can take them into your office. The first step is to check in with yourself (preferably before you meet with a client). Take note of your breathing pattern, style of sitting, tilt of your head, and so forth. After you have grasped your own style, you will be ready to notice when your posture or aspects of your posture match your client's. Also notice your breathing pattern.

Next you can experiment with consciously mimicking the posture (or one aspect of it) of a client. Maybe at first just cross your legs the same way, synchronize your breathing, or put your head in the same position. Once you do that, check in with the elements that were the focus of the previous exercise and see what you come up with. It is not usually a good idea to completely mimic a client's posture when you are sitting face to face. Some clients could feel shamed if they notice.

Most important, check with your client about any hunches. It can be very tempting to assume that the changes in your sensations, emotions, images, or thoughts are accurate details about your client, and they may be. However, they can also be aspects of yourself that have become triggered through the mirroring process. You will not be able to tell the difference unless you check.

If you like the idea, use conscious mirroring as a tool to enhance intuition, but never mistake it for knowledge until you have checked it out with your client.

OTHER APPLICATIONS

You can apply the same idea with others. For example, at dinner, try mimicking the posture of your spouse, friend, or child, and then make some guesses about what they might be feeling or what kind of day they had. You can make a game of it. Conscious mirroring might also be used to help someone who has a low empathy IQ. It could help them learn how it feels to be in another's moccasins for a while.

Postural mirroring can also be a powerful tool for supervision and consultation. Role-playing one of your own clients is an oft-used and valuable technique for gaining insight into a client and revealing areas of countertransference. This same tool is enhanced by paying particular attention to how the client sits and moves. The process is similar to an actor getting into a role. When you can accurately copy the client's bearing and movements, both you and your supervisor will have more hunches to work with.

Unmirroring

[T]hinking of the transmission of moods as akin to the transmission of social viruses, it seems reasonable to suppose that some people . . . stand especially vulnerable to contagion.
—*Hatfield and colleagues* (1994, p. 128)

In the previous section, you learned about using postural mirroring consciously to increase your empathy with a client or other person. Actually the emphasis was on your somatic empathy with that person, as the connection is body to body. For the psychotherapist, that may enhance your resonance with and intuition about your clients. That is the upside of somatic empathy. There is also a downside.

When unchecked, somatic empathy can be problematic. As discussed earlier, unconscious somatic empathy may be a major factor underlying your risk for compassion fatigue, vicarious traumatization, and burnout. However, managing that risk is fairly easy and mainly requires common sense. So-

matic empathy only becomes a danger when the therapist is
not aware of it, and therefore not in control of it, unconsciously tuning into the sensations, emotions, images, and
thoughts of clients. Under that circumstance, the therapist
will not be able to distinguish client states from her own. Actually, it is this confusion that is usually most problematic.

This is a good place to look back at my situation with
Ronald earlier in this chapter (see p. 69). The problem generated for me by postural mirroring was obvious: I confused
Ronald's anger with my own. I mirrored Ronald and then forgot what I had been doing. When I felt rage, I could not locate the source and resolve it, because it had not been generated in response to my own life situation. By accurately
attuning to Ronald, I had picked up—been infected by—his
rage. Had I stayed aware of what I was doing, the distinction
would have been clear to me. However, because I forgot, I
confused the rage infection with a true rage of my own. When
I looked to my own life for the source of my anger, I became
confused and agitated. Once my colleague reminded me of
the postural mirroring I had been doing, the distinction between Ronald and myself—between his feelings and mine—
was instantaneously clear. That difference recognized, the
rage I had adopted melted away. As it dissipated, so did my
discomfort and confusion. It is important to note that unconscious postural mirroring happens all the time in and outside
of therapeutic relationships. The following consultation tran-
script will help illustrate strategies to maintain awareness and
alter habitual unconscious mirroring.

BREATHLESS HANK

*Hank is an experienced psychologist in private practice. He
gets most of his supervision from a peer group, but periodically seeks additional help. During the following consultation, he discussed physical symptoms that had arisen in
working with a particular client.*

Hank: I read your article in the *Networker* [Rothschild, 2004b]. The story you told about losing your breath with a client resonated with my experience with a current client. I hoped you might be able to help me with him and with my reactions.

Consultant: I'll be glad to try. Tell me what happens.

Hank: When I work with this client, about 15 minutes into most sessions, I find myself feeling light-headed. I've noticed that my breathing is very shallow and so is his. I've tried changing my breathing pattern. That works for a few minutes and then I'm light-headed again.

Consultant: Have you looked into content triggers; is what he talks about disturbing for you?

Hank: I did think of that. But this happens no matter what he is talking about. Often we are just addressing his daily life, no sort of distressing material.

It would be ideal to have Hank videotape a session with his client. That way we could look together at what was happening with him. We discussed this idea, but for several reasons, Hank did not think this was possible. Mainly, the client was very concerned about privacy and would probably not give permission. Due to the client's stress level, Hank did not even want to ask. Next I suggested a viable alternative.

Consultant: Then here is what I would like to suggest: I'd like you to imagine that you are in your therapy room with your client. Assume your typical posture, and then observe the image of your client as he talks about various things. I am going to pay attention to what I see in you and may stop you from time to time.

As Hank began to imagine a session with his client, I noticed that he was sitting up fairly straight. A minute or so later, I saw his posture begin to change. He seemed to collapse a bit across his middle and he slid down in the chair.

Consultant: I want to stop you for a moment. I notice something changing in your posture. Can you identify the change? If you can't, I'll tell you what I see, but I want to check first if you can feel it.

Hank: Well, my posture isn't as straight as when I started. Is that what you mean?

Consultant: Yes. Can you describe the difference more precisely?

The more Hank could feel and describe for himself, the better. If I only told him what I saw, he would not gain facility in self-observation. I wanted him to be more able to observe himself during sessions.

Hank: Well, I've slid down in the chair a bit and my head is slightly forward.

Consultant: What's happening in your midsection?

Hank: Oh! I'm sort of folded.

Consultant: That's what I see. To me it looks like you are actually slumping. How is your imagined client sitting?

Hank: Oh, he always slumps!

I was not surprised. It is very common for the therapist to slip into a mirrored posture of the client. Hank inadvertently demonstrated this tendency very well.

Consultant: So, is it possible that as the session continues, you gradually slip into mirroring his slump more and more?

Hank: I guess that's possible. If that's the case, then just changing my breathing wouldn't be enough to help me, would it?

Consultant: Nope. Not only because of the mirroring, but also the actual posture. In that slumped position notice your breathing. Then straighten up, sitting as you were a while ago and see if there is a difference.

Trying out the two postures and focusing on body awareness would help teach Hank's body as well as his mind the difference between the two positions.

Hank: Of course, when I am sitting up straight, it is much easier to breathe deeply. Do you think that it's this simple? Keep from slumping and I'll keep my breath and no longer be light-headed?

Consultant: It may be. What you just said is common sense. At least I think it is worth a try. For the next two sessions, would you pay attention to your posture? It might be difficult to stay out of that mirroring. It looks to be very automatic.

Hank: I'm sure I can do it for two sessions. I'll make a note to myself and post it on my side table.

Two weeks later Hank sent an e-mail to say the change in posture worked very well. He was no longer light-headed with that client. Every time he found himself slumping, he pulled himself up straight again. Unmirroring both his client's breathing pattern and posture worked to keep Hank from being affected by the somatic states of his client.

PUTTING YOU IN CHARGE

Mediating the negative risks of somatic empathy first involves mindfulness: becoming aware of when and how you gain access to information about your clients, how you attune with them, and how you become vulnerable to being infected by their states.

Unmirroring Exercise 1

For the next week, in one or more sessions, pay attention to your own body posture, facial expression, and breathing pattern. Stay alert for times when you drift into patterns that mimic your client.

Occasionally, consciously change one aspect of your position, your breathing, or your expression. Then see whether you feel differently and notice if there is any change in your client.

Most clients will not notice at all. Certain clients will feel more comfortable when you mirror them. However, as mentioned above, many will feel relieved when you do not and are less in tune with them. Many of your clients will be better able to stay in touch with themselves when you stay in touch with yourself.

Unmirroring Exercise 2

This exercise requires a partner. It can be done informally with a friend or colleague, or as part of a group training or consultation. Again, it is not recommended to use this (as written) with clients.

- In pairs, designate one as the client and the other as the therapist.
- The client tells a personal story. It can be about anything with a positive or mildly negative emotional charge, but not trauma or great distress.
- As the therapist listens to the client's story, he consciously mirrors the client's posture, facial expression, or breathing and notices what happens in his own body, emotions, and thoughts.
- Next, the therapist evaluates what he must do to unmirror.
  1. Change his posture?
  2. Change his breathing?
  3. Tense up or relax? Where?
  4. Change position? How?
  5. What else? Feel free to be creative.
- The therapist then shifts between mirroring and unmirroring, taking a minute or two with each. Both

therapist and client notice changes in their own body and emotions as the therapist shifts.

- Finally, let go of the roles and discuss what happened. Usually in this exercise the one in the client role is very sensitive to the therapist's shifts between mirroring and unmirroring.

In your practice, the majority of your clients will not notice whether you are mirroring them or not, at least consciously. So do not hesitate to try unmirroring in actual therapy situations. Of foremost importance is mindfulness (awareness), so that you do not take on client states that will put you at risk. If you worry about unmirroring with your clients, remember: Many clients experience mirrored attunement as intrusive, feeling that they do not have their own space or experience. So feel free to experiment. Use your common sense. If unmirroring helps you to reduce your work stress, use it. If some clients are more uncomfortable when you unmirror, find ways to strike a balance between mirroring and unmirroring. If you do not think it is helpful to you and your clients, use other tools.

Therapists in my training courses have come up with many ways to unmirror. Here are some of their ideas:

Sit up straight

Cross or uncross legs

Change breathing

Take a drink

Write some notes

Stretch

Visit the restroom

Tense specific muscles

Move around

Blink eyes

Take a deep breath

Exhale

The next chapter moves away from the emphasis on empathy but continues to focus on the therapist's body and therapist self-care. Arousal levels and boundaries are additional key components for a psychotherapist to manage in order to mediate the risks of compassion fatigue, vicarious traumatization, and burnout.

Chapter 3

Keeping Calm

T he theory section of this chapter will explain the neurophysiology of arousal, that is what happens in body and brain in states of stress and in states of calm. The skill building section will equip practitioners with tools to guide their own nervous systems to optimal states for their demanding work. The first step is mindfulness achieved through arousal awareness. The second step is to have strategies to reduce stress and hyperarousal, to use therapist's brakes. Finally, the exercise How Close is too Close? will help practitioners to negotiate optimal physical distance between themselves and their clients.

THEORY

The Neurophysiology of Arousal

Chronic stress exacts a great toll on the body and mind. In the psychotherapist, that toll is usually referred to as com-

passion fatigue, vicarious trauma, or burnout. This chapter
reviews the neurophysiological basis for states of both stress
and calm. It also provides tools to enhance your ability to
regulate your own levels of arousal.

No better case can be made for learning about the nervous system and increasing awareness of one's own state of
arousal than the personal story of my colleague Bonnita
Wirth. In her own words (and with her permission):

> After 32 years of direct service, I decided to close my psy-
> chotherapy practice. This was work that I loved and was quite
> successful at for many years. If I had waited much longer to
> make this change, my age would have put me out of the run-
> ning for the kinds of administrative jobs that interested me.
>
> For many, many years (beginning long before middle age)
> I had been a fitful sleeper. I would go to bed late (12:30 A.M.
> or later), wake several times in the night, and was up no later
> than 6:30 A.M. In spite of this, I did not feel tired or notice
> that my lack of sleep was impacting me one way or the other.
> I would sometimes refer to my "insomnia" thinking it was part
> and parcel of who I was. Even a close observer would never
> notice I was suffering any ill effects. I loved my work, en-
> joyed my patients, was successful, and never felt burned out.
> It seemed that my body and mind managed to adjust to the
> rigors of my work; I never noticed. Even the contrast of va-
> cations was not adequate to alert me to the stress I was car-
> rying. I had accommodated to the biological stress and just
> saw the consequences as my unique physiology.
>
> But a year after the closure, I got quite a surprise. I was
> talking about the changes over the past year with a colleague
> and reflected that within weeks of closing my practice, I
> started sleeping through the night *for the first time in over
> three decades*. This was an astonishing revelation and the
> first time I realized the connection. For all of those years I
> had never considered that my chosen and beloved profession
> had a cost: a significant impact on my body, my sleep, and
> my ability to fully relax. Having trouble falling asleep, sleep-
> ing fitfully, and waking had become my norm.

With that insight, I began to notice what had changed. I actually relaxed and felt tired when I got home from work. My nights are very different now: I am drifting off by 10 or 11 P.M., sleep solidly and peacefully, and first awaken at 5:30 A.M. or later. Amazing!

I can't imagine what it must be like for those who are really burned out, burdened with compassion fatigue, or reeling from vicarious trauma.

Bonnita Wirth, Ph.D., September 2004

THE AUTONOMIC NERVOUS SYSTEM

Knowledge of the body is relevant for any psychotherapist. However, some will not be able to study all of it, and some will not be interested. If you only have time or brain space for the most valuable bit of physiology, this is it. At the very least, becoming familiar with the autonomic division of the body's nervous system (ANS) is a must for those who work with highly distressed or traumatized people. Grasping the ANS will provide key tools for both client containment and therapist self-care. Applications for clients are covered at length in *The Body Remembers: The Psychophysiology of Trauma and Trauma Treatment* (Rothschild, 2000). Here the emphasis is on applications for the therapist.

The ANS is at the center of the body's response to stress. It is the ANS that prepares the body for fight, flight, or freeze when faced with a threat to life or limb. Lesser levels of arousal prepare the body to meet any demand—also those of difficult clients or workplaces. The racing heartbeat, cold sweat, and dry mouth associated with the effects of stress are all functions of the ANS. Likewise, the relaxed respiration, warm and dry skin, and lowered blood pressure associated with feelings of calm are also functions of the ANS. Understanding how the ANS works, and being able to identify the internal interoceptive cues that differentiate stress from relaxation, are critical for the therapist working with, and in proximity to, stress and trauma. The advantages extend beyond

helping others. As, or even more, important is the benefit to
the psychotherapist himself. Knowledge about the ANS can
be used to protect you from major job risks: compassion fatigue, vicarious traumatization, and burnout.

It is not only during a traumatic event that the ANS activates toward fight, flight, or freeze, nor is it only the ANS of
the victim that is vulnerable to activation. The therapist working with highly stressed or traumatized individuals is vulnerable to heightened activation of the ANS, even when just sitting in an office and talking with a client. Vicarious trauma is
a reality. Shindul-Rothschild (2001; no relation to the author)
reported, "14% of mental health practitioners working with
trauma victims reported traumatic stress levels similar to those
experienced by victims with PTSD." The therapist who can
track ANS activation in her own body is in a position to
choose the amount of arousal that she can manage or use to
her advantage. She then also has the potential to halt or decrease her arousal, at will, to prevent adverse effects.

Basic Functions

Simply put, the ANS has two branches, the sympathetic nervous system (SNS) and the parasympathetic nervous system
(PNS). They function in balance to promote survival of the
individual and maintain homeostasis within the body. The
SNS activates under conditions of stress, of which traumatic
stress is the most extreme. The PNS is usually activated during rest and relaxation, though it is also active when some distressing feelings such as sadness occur. It can be elevated to
hyperarousal when we feel shame, embarrassment, anger (not
rage), and extreme terror, as is discussed below. Normally the
SNS and PNS arouse and subdue, rise and fall, in complement
to each other. Like the pans of a scale—when one is more activated, the other is more suppressed. Neither branch ever
ceases to function.

When the SNS is primarily aroused, heart rate and respiration quicken, pupils dilate, blood pressure rises, blood flow is

directed away from the skin and viscera into the muscles, and digestion slows or stops. All of this action is nature's way of helping the body respond to demands. When quick and strong movements are needed, the bulk of the blood flow—with the nutrients and oxygen it carries—is directed to the muscles. Increased respiration ensures a greater supply of oxygen, and a quicker heart rate speeds it on its way. Nothing is wasted on the temporarily less important function of digestion, so the mouth goes dry as saliva is no longer needed. Warmth is also a lower priority, so the skin becomes cold and pale as the blood also flows away from it. The pupils dilate so that distance vision—toward the source of danger or goal of safety—is more acute. When threat is extreme, the bowel and bladder might empty, making the body lighter for quicker action, as well as leaving scent-rich scat to distract a pursuer.

The PNS is usually most aroused in states of rest and relaxation. The heartbeat and respiration slow, blood pressure lowers, pupils constrict, and the skin is warm and dry. When the PNS is dominant, much of the blood flow is directed away from the muscles, as their action is not as important. Instead, blood is directed toward the skin for warmth and the viscera to process nutrition through digestion and elimination. The mouth is wet with saliva, which, along with chewing, is necessary to begin the digestive process.

Under the most extreme life-threatening danger, the SNS and PNS might be simultaneously hyperaroused to their most extreme level, pushing all systems to full throttle and causing the body to freeze—go dead like a mouse caught by a cat, or a deer or kangaroo caught in headlights. Figure 3.1, reproduced from *The Body Remembers* (Rothschild, 2000), summarizes the features of SNS and PNS activation.

How the ANS Responds to Trauma

The ANS is controlled by the brain's limbic system. It is this neural structure that coordinates or directs survival of the

FIGURE 3.1 COMPARISON OF SYMPATHETIC AND PARASYMPATHETIC AROUSAL*

AUTONOMIC NERVOUS SYSTEM (ANS)
(smooth muscles)
(involuntary)

SYMPATHETIC BRANCH (SNS)	PARASYMPATHETIC BRANCH (PNS)
Activates during positive *and* negative stress states, including sexual climax, rage, desperation, terror, anxiety/panic, trauma	States of activation include rest and relaxation, sexual arousal, happiness, anger, grief, sadness
Noticeable signs: Faster respiration Quicker heart rate (pulse) Increased blood pressure Pupils dilate Pale skin color Increased sweating Skin cold (possibly clammy) Digestion (and peristalsis) decreases	**Noticeable signs:** Slower, deeper respiration Slower heart rate (pulse) Decreased blood pressure Pupils constrict Flushed skin color Skin dry (usually warm) to touch Digestion (and peristalsis) increases
During actual traumatic event OR with flashback (visual, auditory, and/or sensory): Preparation for quick movement, leading to possible fight reflex or flight reflex	**During actual traumatic event OR with flashback (visual, auditory, and/or sensory):** Can also activate concurrently with, while masking, sympathetic activation, leading to tonic immobility: freezing reflex (like a mouse, caught by a cat, going dead). Marked by simultaneous signs of high sympathetic and parasympathetic activation.

Source: Rothschild, 2000.

* Stephen Porges has evolved an alternative understanding of the ANS and the reflexes of fight, flight, and freeze that has become popular in recent years (1995, 2003). In his *polyvagal theory,* Porges proposes that the freeze response is mediated by the dorsal branch of the *vagus* nerve. He rejects the idea that the freeze response is the result of simultaneous hyperarousal of the SNS and PNS. Porges further rejects the concept of the PNS altogether, replacing it with ventral vagal activation that enables *social interaction.* Though compelling, Porges's arguments are not sufficient for me to abandon the current understanding of the freeze response as described here. Neither can I dismiss the existence of the PNS as it is still the most comprehensive concept available for the neurophysiological identification of states of calm. I still firmly believe that familiarization with the indicators of SNS and PNS activation is the best tool available for monitoring a client's and one's own states of stress and calm. Remember, you want to *avoid* freeze. Tracking PNS/SNS arousal will make that possible. No matter which theory you subscribe to, being able to identify and distinguish SNS and PNS activation—per this table—in your own body is one of your very best hedges against compassion fatigue, vicarious traumatization, and burnout.

species, including the management of all levels of stress. The limbic system makes sure that food is sought when there is hunger, that liquid is found for thirst, that urges for sex are consummated so that the species continues to propagate. The limbic system also controls the stress response and directs the body to fight, flee, or freeze when faced with danger.

A small almond-shaped structure within the brain's limbic system, the amygdala, is responsible for all types of emotional response. It is best known for its role in perceiving danger. It gathers information from the sensory system—exteroceptors and interoceptors—and sounds an alarm. When that happens, a whole sequence of further activations ensues within the body. An alarm from the amygdala activates the hypothalamus, setting in motion two parallel actions: One activates the SNS while the other provokes the pituitary gland. The SNS triggers the adrenals to release epinephrine and norepinephrine, which mobilize the body for fight or flight. The pituitary action also stimulates the adrenals to release something different: cortisol. Following a successful fight or flight, cortisol will quiet the amygdala's alarm and return the nervous system to a state of homeostasis.

At least, that is how the system functions under ideal circumstances. Difficulties can develop in this sequence, however, when fight or flight are not successful, or if they are not possible. Under such circumstances, the amygdala continues to sound an alarm; the SNS continues to activate and prepare the body for fight or flight. The result is what I identify as the hallmarks of post-traumatic stress disorder (PTSD): Persistent symptoms of hyperarousal in the ANS. These include hyperstartle response, hypervigilance, difficulty staying asleep, and others listed for PTSD in the *DSM-IV* (American Psychiatric Association, 1994).

Another difficulty can occur. When, under extreme threat, neither fight nor flight is possible, the limbic system can direct the body, instead, to go into a state of freeze, sometimes called *tonic immobility* (Gallup & Maser, 1977). Exactly how the freeze response occurs is not as well understood as fight and flight. Many researchers have found (and I concur) that it results from a simultaneous activation of the PNS and the SNS. When that happens, features of hyperarousal of the SNS (rapid heartbeat and respiration; cold, humid skin; pupil dilation; and raised blood pressure) persist while features of hyperarousal of the PNS (highly flushed skin, very slow respiration and heart rate, constricted pupils, and a drop in blood pressure) will also be present. This state can be identified by indicators of SNS hyperarousal (e.g., extremely rapid heart rate, very dry mouth) that occur with indicators of PNS hyperarousal (e.g., extremely slow respiration, very flushed skin)—a hodgepodge.

Freezing is characterized by paralysis, with either slack muscles (as when a mouse is captured by a cat) or stiff muscles (like a deer or kangaroo caught in headlights). During freezing there is an altered sense of time and space, reduced registration of pain, and dampened emotion. Those who have frozen under threat report a kind of dissociative experience: Time slows down and they are no longer afraid. As such, freezing is also an extremely valuable survival defense. However, it has greater consequences in the aftermath of trauma than does either fight or flight. Studies demonstrate that those who dissociate during trauma (including freezing) have a greater chance of developing PTSD than those who do not (Bremner et al., 1992; Classen, Koopman, & Spiegel, 1993; Shalev, Peri, Canetti, & Schreiber, 1996).

 It is important to note that an individual does not have the luxury of choosing whether he responds to threat with fight, flight, or freezing responses. It is a subcortical (i.e., not thought out), automatic response mediated by the limbic system of the brain. There is no shame in freezing. It is the limbic system's best strategy for survival based on instantaneous evaluation of each situation and each person's unique resources and circumstances.

THE ANS, SOMATIC EMPATHY, AND VICARIOUS TRAUMA

Therapists working with very stressed and traumatized individuals are at particularly high risk for compassion fatigue or vicarious trauma when they ignore or are unable to distinguish their own symptoms of SNS arousal. This common therapist hazard, however, is not necessary; it can be prevented, or at least greatly reduced.

We are most vulnerable to compassion fatigue and vicarious traumatization when we are unaware of the state of our own body and mind. We can become so focused on the distress of those in our care that we neglect our own growing discomfort. Actually, as Bonnita Wirth found, we can even miss or misread the indicators that would tell us we are generally under stress. Sometimes it might be that your body is screaming in pain, fright, or exhaustion and you do not heed the signs. Of course there can be circumstances under which the needs of a client must supersede your own, but these should be rare instances. If you are to be able to continue to help your clients and take care of yourself, you have to learn to watch for and recognize signals which tell you that you need to take a break, to rest, to talk to someone about your own experiences, to be with family and friends, to cry, to regroup, and so on. What are those signals and how do you recognize them?

Identifying ANS Arousal—Both SNS and PNS

In *The Body Remembers* (Rothschild, 2000), I promoted the use of body awareness to help trauma therapy clients learn to identify and track their own states of ANS arousal. Learning these basics helps clients toward greater control over their arousal states.

The same idea is relevant to and highly recommended for psychotherapists as well. Forester (2001) compared therapists who regularly practiced body awareness during clinical encounters with those who did not. She found that the frequency of attention to body awareness was a significant variable. In those clinicians who indicated lower incidence of vicarious traumatization, body awareness was the key. In addition, a preliminary investigation by Rothschild, Shiffrar, and Turner (2005) has indicated that body awareness is critical for mediating the risks of vicarious trauma and burnout (see Appendix 2 for a more detailed description of this project.) Again, common sense! The more adept you become at recognizing, tracking, and evaluating the level of arousal in your own body, the better you will be able to regulate your arousal and mediate your own risks for compassion fatigue, vicarious trauma, and burnout.)

The first step is to become familiar with the features of SNS and PNS arousal as outlined in Figure 3.1. For some, first focusing on your own responses may come easier. Other individuals will learn this most easily by first observing arousal changes in others—clients, family, and friends—just to get attuned to observing it. Discover how you learn best. Once your observation skills are developed, they can be turned inward. Sometimes the intricacies of ANS arousal are most easily grasped in groups. Some readers may find it useful to get together with one or more colleagues and learn this together. If working with peers, take turns with the exercises in the next section. Observe each other one at a time and discuss what you see. Then the person who is being observed can give feedback on her own body awareness—a chance to develop skills of observation and self-awareness simultaneously. A major potential for preventing and healing compassion fatigue and vicarious trauma is tied to your ability to recognize sensations that signal hyperarousal in you.

Using breathing as an example, what might distinguish breathing driven by the PNS from that which is driven by the SNS? PNS breathing tends to be slow, long breaths, which go deep into the lungs, causing them to expand downward and the belly to puff out. In PNS breathing, the emphasis is on the exhale, sometimes even a sigh. SNS breathing, on the other hand, tends to come in quicker gasps with an emphasis on the inhale. SNS breathing is usually restricted to the upper chest.

Now, of course, I have described two extremes. Normal breathing for most people lies somewhere between those extremes. The idea, though, is to learn your own pattern of relaxed, resting breathing, and to identify how that is different from your breathing when you are mildly stressed and when you are highly stressed. That way you will have indicators of when you might be at risk. Then you will be in a position to intercede.

In Sync With Our Clients

Many studies have looked at ANS synchrony between people. In fact, Levenson and Ruef (1997) devoted 10 full pages to a review of that literature in their book chapter, "Physiological Aspects of Emotional Knowledge and Rapport." Even synchronized heart rates between therapists and clients have been studied (Coleman, Greenblatt, & Solomon, 1956; DiMascio, Boyd, Greenblatt, & Solomon, 1955; Stanek, Hahn, & Mayer, 1973). Especially interesting is DiMascio, Boyd, and Greenblatt's 1957 study. They identified a direct concordance between the heart rates of therapists and those of their clients as the tension level of the therapy sessions fluctuated. However, they also found that heart rates were inversely related when the client was feeling antagonistic toward the therapist—somatic empathy versus somatic antipathy, so to speak.

Levenson and Ruef went on to question the veracity of the aforementioned studies, cautioning that they were prone to methodological problems. Nonetheless, many therapists will recognize this kind of cardiac synchrony in their own experience with clients. Sometimes the therapist's first hint that a client is becoming anxious is a quickening of the therapist's own heartbeat or breathing. Many psychotherapists already know that one way to calm a client's panic attack is to breathe slowly themselves. The panicked client will often, unconsciously, synchronize his breathing, slowing it and becoming calmer in the process.

Autonomic synchrony is one of the core components of somatic empathy. As such, it is critical to be able to recognize it in yourself. Sometimes you will want to be in autonomic sync with your clients; it might help you know them on a deeper level. However, more often it could threaten your own well-being. The first step to controlling this synchrony is to become aware of its nuances and to evaluate for yourself when it is productive and when it could be risky for you. Exercises toward that goal follow.

SKILL BUILDING

Arousal Awareness

Simple body awareness is the single most useful tool for identifying levels of arousal—those that are beneficial and those that threaten good functioning. It is at least as, if not more, important for therapists than it is for their clients. Refer back to Figure 3.1. All of those indicators of ANS arousal, both SNS and PNS, will be useful for you to memorize and be able to identify in your own body.

Simple body and arousal awareness is a useful skill in itself. As mentioned before, Forester (2001) found that body awareness alone could lower the incidence of vicarious traumatization. It can also serve as a baseline for evaluating the effectiveness of other skills. You can check your awareness before you try an intervention and then check in after you have made a change. That way you can determine more precisely how and whether any particular skill or change works for you.

In the following exercises, you will first be guided in developing awareness of your body. That awareness will serve as a basis for identifying your arousal level. Next, you will be introduced to skills that will aid you in controlling your levels of arousal in and outside of therapy sessions. Finally, using your body and arousal awareness, you will learn skills that will help you to evaluate and increase bodily boundaries where appropriate for you. This set of skills is progressive; each builds on the ones that precede it. Therefore it is recommended that you practice each step in order.

EXERCISE 1: SIMPLE BODY AWARENESS

In a quiet room at a peaceful time, try this exercise: Sit comfortably and take notice of what you become most aware of in your body. Identify the temperature and humidity on the surface of your skin. Is it warm and dry, cool and moist, or something in between? Notice that there are differences depending on where your skin is clothed or bare. There will also be differences depending on how your blood is circulating at the moment. Remember that some people tend toward cold feet or hands.

Next, notice where you are tense and where you are relaxed. Look for nuances of difference throughout your body (upper body versus lower body, right to left, etc.). What about your breathing? Is it deep or shallow, high or low? Also, notice how the expression on your face feels from the inside. What is the position and expression of your mouth, eyes, forehead? Can you feel your heart? Is it beating fast or slow?

These are some of the areas of awareness that will help guide you to identify your arousal level and estimate if it is going to remain manageable for you. You will find that some areas of your body are more easily accessed by your awareness than others. Discover the somatic cues that are most available to you, and exercise the ones that are more difficult.

Next, remember something pleasant from your life. Notice any changes in skin, muscles, face, breathing, and heartbeat. Just take note of the changes. You can write them down if you would like to.

Then, remember something slightly unpleasant from your life, or think about something you are anticipating with mild anxiety or irritation. Again, note changes in the areas mentioned above.

Finally, vacillate back and forth between pleasant and unpleasant memories or anticipations, a few seconds with each. This will help to hone your awareness of changes in your body systems. In this way, when you are not under any pressure, you can develop your skill in body and arousal awareness. The more you practice, the greater the chance that this knowledge will be available to you in actual stressful situations.

EXERCISE 2: BODY AWARENESS IN SESSION

Once you have a feel for what it means to be aware of your body, you can take that into the therapy session. Begin this practice with a client who is fairly easy to work with. Since learning any new skill takes some degree of focus, it would not be wise to begin with your most demanding client. Once you feel comfortable attending to your body sensations during a session with one or two easier clients, you will be able to begin using the same skills with more difficult clients.

When therapy sessions are engaging, it is sometimes difficult to remember to pay attention to your own body. It can be helpful to place something within your usual line of sight that can remind you to check in with your body from time to time. It can be a symbol or a word. Often a file card does the trick. It really does not matter as long as you recognize its meaning.

Once that reminder is in place, during a session with your chosen client, once every 15 to 20 minutes tune into your own body and assess for the distribution of temperature and tension differences, your breathing pattern, facial expression, position of your limbs, and so on per Exercise 1 above. Notice if and how some of these elements change throughout the session. At this point, put aside your interest in what the changes might mean. This step is just for developing awareness. The additional exercises in this chapter and following chapters build upon that base.

EXERCISE 3: TRACKING AROUSAL

The better you are able to gauge your own levels of ANS arousal, the better you will be able to care for yourself in— and following—therapy sessions. Arousal awareness is a skill. Like any skill, it takes practice. It will be made easier by mastering the basics of body awareness, as in Exercises 1 and 2.

The ANS is not your only usable gauge. It may also be useful to notice what else is happening in your body: sleeping patterns, stomach upset, changes in vision or hearing, and so forth. Changes in those habits may be indicative of chronic changes in ANS arousal and are worthwhile to track for their own sake. (Bonnita Wirth may have benefited from such attention to her sleep patterns, for example, noticing how they changed when she went into private practice. Had she done so, she may have noticed sooner that her body was not optimally managing the stress of her work.) Monitoring your ANS will be your most direct tool for judging when you are managing things well and when you are not, both over time and from moment to moment.

As has been said, though, it takes practice. First you need to become familiar with the signs of sympathetic and parasympathetic arousal as described in the previous section. Memorize them if you can. Then, during a normal day, check in with yourself from time to time and pay particular attention to your heart rate, respiration, skin humidity, and temperature. Learn what is normal for you when you are relaxed or not particularly under stress. You can also learn what is normal for you under conditions of moderate stress. Once you know your own tendencies, you will have the possibility of differentiating your safety zone from your danger zone.

Below is a general description of states of ANS arousal. These descriptors are meant to serve as a guide, not as an evaluation tool. The list is modified from Rothschild (2000).

- *Relaxed system*—primarily moderate activation of PNS. Breathing is easy and deep, heart rate slow, skin warm and dry. A relaxed system indicates you are calm and fairly comfortable.

- *Slight arousal*—signs of low to moderate PNS activation combined with slightly rising SNS activation. Breathing or heart rate may quicken while skin color remains normal; skin may cool and moisten slightly without increases in respiration and pulse, and so on. Slight arousal indicates excitement or containable discomfort.

- *Moderate hyperarousal*—primarily signs of increased SNS arousal. This includes rapid heartbeat, rapid respiration, skin becoming cool, possibly moist, and so forth. Moderate arousal may mean you are having trouble dealing with what is going on and may be quite anxious; it may be time to slow things down, to apply the brakes (see the next section).

- *Severe hyperarousal*—primarily signs of very high SNS arousal. Signs include accelerated heartbeat, accelerated respiration, pale skin tone, cold sweat, and so on. Severe arousal is a sign that it is time to hit the brakes wherever possible.

- *Endangering hyperarousal*—signs of very high activation of both SNS and PNS. For example, pale (or reduced color) skin (SNS) with slow heartbeat (PNS); widely dilated pupils (SNS) with flushed color (PNS); slow heart rate (PNS) with rapid breathing (SNS); very slow respiration (PNS) with fast heart beat (SNS).

Endangering arousal is a sign that you are at high risk. You may be about to panic, dissociate, or freeze. At this point it is necessary to slam on the brakes. One purpose of learning to observe the bodily signs of ANS arousal is to become com petent in avoiding this highly risky (and possibly traumatizing) state, slowing down before that state is reached.

EXERCISE 4: TRACKING AROUSAL DURING SESSIONS

This exercise will guide you in tracking your level of ANS arousal during a therapy session with a client. Paying attention to your arousal level will help you know how your own system is managing what is going on in the session. For a multitude of reasons, a client's therapy session can adversely affect the therapist. All too often, when that happens the therapist does not know about it until after the session. Sometimes the aftereffects can be debilitating. By tracking your ANS, warnings of a possible difficulty can be identified during the session, enabling immediate intervention. That way, you will have more choices for managing your client work with fewer ill effects.

Tracking your arousal during a therapy session follows from what you learned in Exercise 2. Arousal awareness is just one, albeit specialized, form of body awareness. Again, it is advisable to begin your practice with a less-demanding client. It is possible that with such a client shifts in your arousal may be less dramatic, but tracking them will still help you get used to the process.

As with the exercise for simple body awareness, post a file card or some other object within your line of sight to help remind you to pay attention to your arousal level. (When I was learning this, I wrote "ANS" in red on a white card and pinned it to the wall behind my client chair.) For the first few sessions, it will be more than enough to scan your arousal level two to three times during a session. Rather than general body awareness, you will be specifically focusing on skin temperature and humidity, particularly in your hands and feet, along with heart rate, respiration rate, and how wet or dry your mouth is. Further, it is a good idea to notice just how much in contact you are with your body, your surroundings, and your client. Losing a sense of yourself or the room you are in can be a sign of dissociation, which would indicate severe or endangering hyperarousal. You may not be able to identify dissociation once you are in it, but it is possible to learn to read the signs that you are on your way there (as someone with epilepsy can learn to predict a seizure).

Once you gain confidence in tracking your arousal with a less challenging client, you will be ready to try the same with a client who is more emotionally demanding for you. The same principles apply: several times during a session, check in with your body and gauge your arousal. An opportune time for this is when you are encouraging the same from your client. When you ask him about his body awareness or arousal level, you can be checking yours at the same time.

Now that you can track your arousal level, you will want tools for regulating it. In the next section, strategies for lowering arousal are applied to the needs of the distressed therapist during psychotherapy sessions with clients. Conveniently, many of the same strategies will also work for your clients, but the focus here is on you.

The Therapist's Brakes

The idea of "putting on the brakes" for managing the rigors of trauma therapy was first put forward in *The Body Remembers: The Psychophysiology of Trauma and Trauma Treatment* (Rothschild, 2000). There the theory and strategies were geared to enhancing the client's control over the debilitating symptoms of PTSD and for keeping trauma therapy at a digestible pace for each client. The same theory and most of the strategies may be just as useful as an aid for clients with other types of problems, particularly anxiety and panic.

Conveniently, and most relevant for the topic of this book, the same theory and skills for applying client brakes are extremely useful for psychotherapist brakes. Of course, for psychotherapists, brakes are particularly useful for reducing in-session hyperarousal and protecting against the direct impact of client material. Paying attention to levels of arousal and putting on the brakes will help therapists monitor and manage their own vulnerability to compassion fatigue, vicarious traumatization, and burnout on a day-to-day, session-to-session basis.

To use brakes effectively, it is suggested that you first become familiar with the theory of ANS arousal and attain a degree of arousal awareness, as described in the previous sections. The idea is to be able to identify ANS arousal in yourself and then to be able to apply the brakes to keep it within the range that is optimal for you. That means that you can reduce arousal when it becomes too high, and also that you can allow it to rise when that enhances your drive, assertiveness, follow-through, and so on. In this section, however, I stick to the discussion of using brakes to lower arousal.

The following case illustration will give you an idea of what putting on the brakes may look like when applied to the needs of the therapist. Instruction in specific braking skills follows.

Elena is a clinical social worker in a family service agency. She sees a wide variety of clients: males and females of various sexual orientations, ages, and types of presenting problems. One of her long-term clients, a 63-year-old man, is facing the loss of his wife of 30 years; she is terminally ill. For the last few months, as her client's grief has risen to the surface, Elena has been having symptoms of anxiety during and following their sessions. Elena knows the basis of her countertransference: Her own mother died 2 years ago—at nearly the same age as her client's wife— after a long illness. Elena is still feeling the loss. She isn't suffering posttraumatic stress, simply grief. However, that knowledge alone has not been adequate to reduce the heart palpitations and shortness of breath that are triggered as she helps her client with his grief. Though she attends grief counseling and is making headway, she needs a stopgap measure to help in the interim. She wants to continue working with her client, but without increasing her own discomfort.

During a regularly scheduled meeting, the agency supervisor asked Elena to describe, with as much detail as she could, what happened to her during sessions with her client.

"For the first few weeks, I would become anxious during the sessions. Now, actually, my anxiety begins before the session in anticipation. As I am walking to the waiting room to get him, my heart races and my hands and feet go cold. This has really become a bad pattern. Generally, I'm at least somewhat anxious the whole session. After he leaves, I'm a bit shaky for a few minutes, but writing up session notes helps me to calm down." The supervisor latched onto that last comment. It is relevant that Elena already has a tool for bringing down her arousal before she sees her next client. Logically, since that tool works, it is likely that others will also.

The supervisor and Elena spent the next half hour experimenting with a few tools for putting on the brakes described in the next few pages: muscle toning, distance boundaries, and body armor. They discovered several that look promising to help Elena, and she agreed to try one or more before and during the next session with her client.

The following week, prior to meeting her client, Elena felt the usual anxiety. Her heartbeat accelerated and the temperature of her hands decreased. Per the supervisor's assignment, this time Elena spent a couple of minutes increasing muscle tone in her arms (one of the techniques she and the supervisor found to be most helpful). She realized it was working as she noticed her hands warming up and her heartbeat slowing a bit. When she brought her client back to her office, Elena made a point of moving her own chair back about a foot more than usual—preoccupied by his grief, the client appeared not to notice. During the session, Elena continued to monitor her arousal and anxiety (as discussed a few pages back). About halfway through the session, her heartbeat began to quicken. Again Elena increased tension in her arms (as shown in the following exercises) and then wrote a few sentences on her notepad and left it on her lap. The notepad provided something for her hands to hold onto and also a small barrier between her and the client. As a result, Elena's anxiety lowered and she was able to complete the session effectively. Following the session, she had some mild anxiety, but nothing like the high levels following previous sessions.

Simple tools helped Elena to reduce anxiety and continue working with her client. Sometimes it is just that simple. However, each practitioner will have to discover which tools work best, and under which conditions. Several are introduced in the next section.

USING BRAKES

This intriguingly relevant e-mail was sent to me in 2004. The author has given me permission to print it and identify her:

> Dear Babette,
>
> I recently started working as a counselor at a rehab for recovering addicts. The suffering there is unlike any I have come across before. I found myself overwhelmed. This was in conflict with my ideals . . . to resonate with another's pain. I recently realized that I wasn't feeling compassion, or even empathy by resonating. I was feeling what in Buddhism is called "horrified anxiety." So this started me thinking about how I can "put on the brakes."
>
> Sharon Collins, Norfolk, England

The discussion and skills that follow should help to address Sharon's concern of how to put on the brakes.

This section focuses on skills that are specifically geared to lowering ANS arousal and putting on the brakes in the moment. By now you may also have realized that you already do things that effectively put on your brakes. However, when those tools are not enough (or do not work for you), one of these may help.

The question of when to put on the brakes is somewhat individual and best answered using the guidelines in the earlier description of ANS states. The commonsense questions are: Where do you function best? Are you at your most competent when your system is relaxed? Do you function better when you are slightly aroused? It is doubtful that any psychotherapist functions well when arousal is severe, and certainly endangering hyperarousal is to be avoided in client and therapist alike. You will probably find that your arousal levels vary from day to day, client to client, and topic to topic. How often you use a tool for applying the brakes will depend on how effectively a tool works for you and how often you check in with yourself to evaluate your arousal level. For instance, on a day when you are feeling well and calm to begin with, you might monitor your arousal only once or twice in a session. But on a day when you are agitated, or when faced with personal or work stress, or particularly distressing client material, it might be a good idea to take stock several times in a session. If you have difficulty keeping a dual focus (you and your client at the same time), you might take time to evaluate your own state when you ask your client to evaluate hers.

When under stress, you may find that just focusing on your body (as you did in the Arousal Awareness section), becoming aware of your heart rate, breathing, skin, muscles, and face, will be enough to reduce anxiety and maintain an optimal level of arousal. Simple body awareness alone often makes arousal more manageable. When body awareness is not adequate, you may find some of the skills that follow to be useful additions.

RELAXED VERSUS CALM

Muscle tension, sometimes regarded as a foe, is in fact a loyal friend of containment and stress management. Just ask your neighborhood police or firefighters. One of the usual ways they and others in high-stress jobs manage pressure is with weight lifting, regular workouts, and sports. Keeping the body muscularly fit is as important as relaxation, adequate rest, and good nutrition for handling stress. Obviously, some types of chronic muscle tension can be uncomfortable, even debilitating. In those instances, relaxation through massage, hot baths, muscle stretching, progressive muscle relaxation, and so on may be very helpful. But do not underestimate the benefit of good muscle tone—you could not hold up this book or do much of anything else without it.

The goal of putting on the brakes is to become calmer so that you can think clearly. (This concept is expanded on in the next chapter, "Thinking Clearly.") Calm and relaxed are not necessarily the same thing. Relaxation involves loose muscles; calm is indicated by low ANS arousal. Therefore, increasing relaxation may be contraindicated for on-the-job stress that requires a high level of functioning. Consider that some muscle tension might actually be "friendly tension," helping you to better manage the demands of your personal and professional lives.

A small body of research suggests that relaxation can actually increase anxiety in some people (Heide & Borkovec, 1983; Jacobsen, 1974; Lehrer & Woolfolk, 1993). You can use body awareness to identify whether you fall into that category. If so, you will want to actually avoid relaxation techniques when you are stressed and favor increasing muscle tone. The best way to find out is to experiment: Try working with relaxation a couple of times when you are highly stressed. Then try increasing your muscle tone a couple of times (instruction follows). Evaluate the results based on which strategy helped you be the most functional, calm, and clear-headed, *not* the most relaxed.

Increasing muscle tone is easy enough. Most forms of exercise will enhance tone. It is a good idea to combine body awareness with exercise (or any other of these skills, for that matter) to be able to discover precisely which exercises will be most useful for your own stress management. Get into a regular exercise program: Use the machines at the gym or free weights at home, walk, swim, bicycle, or something else. Discover where additional muscle tone might shore you up emotionally. When using muscle tone for this purpose, it can be important to stop exercise short of muscular exhaustion. Sometimes at my gym I notice people exercising until they are nauseated or nearly passing out. Their bodies are signaling that they have gone too far, but they are not listening; the slogan "Do it till it burns" echoes in their ears. Follow the wisdom of your body and stop when you begin to be tired, while the exercise still feels good. That way you will look forward to, rather than dread, the next time.

In the Danish Bodynamic training program (Copenhagen, 1988–1992), I learned their theory about a relationship between specific muscle strength and managing stress and assertiveness. Though there is no research on their hypothesis, you can try for yourself to see if strengthening specific muscles helps you out. For example, when you find yourself under stress:

- *Do you lack "backbone"? Is it hard for you to stand up for yourself?* If so, you might try to strengthening the long muscles of your back and neck, so that it is easier to hold your torso and head upright. Laying flat on your stomach and slowly lifting your head can help to increase tone in the muscles along your spine and neck. Sitting up straight will also strengthen those muscles.
- *Are you prone to "go weak in the knees" when you are surprised, frightened, or stressed?* Adding strength to your thighs may help. Knee bends or skiing exercises can help develop stronger knees.
- *Have you noticed yourself having trouble "standing on your own two feet," not able to make decisions or do things on your own?* Strengthening the muscles in your lower legs may help. Try exercises that flex the ankle, working the muscles on the backs of your calves.

- *Is it difficult to be assertive, to say "no" or "stop"?* Doing push-ups to add strength to your arms' triceps may prove useful.
- *Is it difficult to "hold yourself together" under stress?* Increasing tone along the outsides of your thighs may help. Side leg lifts are particularly useful for this.

It may also be handy to be able to increase muscle tone in the face of immediate stress, to put on the brakes. For that purpose, exercises from Rothschild (2000) are reproduced here. They can be used as described or used to inspire you to find other muscles to tense that will benefit you in a pinch.

TENSING PERIPHERAL MUSCLES

It is important to note that any tensing should be done only until the muscle feels slightly tired. Releasing the tension must be done slowly. This is not progressive muscle relaxation. The idea here is to try to maintain a little of the contraction or tension. Try one exercise and evaluate it with body awareness before going on to the next. If tensing causes any adverse reaction (nausea, spaceyness, anxiety, etc.), you can usually neutralize that reaction by gently stretching the same muscle—making an opposite movement (Bodynamic Institute, 1988).

Side of Legs

Stand with feet a little less than shoulder-width apart, knees relaxed (neither locked nor bent). Press knees out directly to the side so that you can feel tension along the sides of the legs (if you are wearing slacks, along the seam) from knee to hip (Bodynamic Institute, 1988).

Left Arm

Sit or stand with arms crossed right over left. The right hand should be covering the left elbow.

The right hand provides resistance as the left arm lifts directly away from the body. You should feel tension in the forward-directed part of the upper arm from shoulder to elbow.

The right hand provides resistance to the back of the elbow as the left arm pushes directly to the left. You should feel tension in the left-directed part of the upper arm from shoulder to elbow (Robyn Bohen, personal communication, April 1991).

Right Arm

Sit or stand with arms crossed left over right. The left hand should be covering the right elbow.

The left hand provides resistance as the right arm lifts directly away from the body. You should feel tension in the forward-directed part of the upper arm from shoulder to elbow.

The left hand provides resistance to the back of the elbow as the right arm pushes directly right. You should feel tension in the right-directed part of the upper arm from shoulder to elbow (Robyn Bohen, personal communication, April 1991).

Thigh Tensing

Sitting in a chair, place both feet flat on the floor. Press weight onto your feet just until you feel tension build in your thighs.

There should be no risk to experimenting with the different muscle toning exercises *as long as* you use your own awareness to determine which exercises are OK for you to use (the ones that increase calm and clear thinking) and which you should bypass (the ones that result in anxiety, spaciness, and cloudy thinking).

SENSORY ANCHORS

The idea of an anchoring "safe place" was first introduced for use with hypnosis (Napier, 1996). Since then, it has been adapted for use with psychotherapy clients as a tool of many methods of therapy, particularly trauma therapy. The technique usually involves accessing memories that are associated with support and safety. The strategy of using an anchor is particularly useful for the psychotherapist himself—during or outside of therapy—to put on his own brakes. An effective anchor should be able to reduce hyperarousal quickly.

Traditionally, anchoring techniques utilize visual imagery. Here that idea is extended to include an emphasis on all aspects of sensory awareness to enhance the effect of the calming memory. In addition, the concept is refined and linked to the body. That will make it possible for the *feel* of an anchor to be kindled quickly, at will, whether in the midst of a stressful session or to mediate episodes of compassion fatigue or vicarious traumatization at other times. An effective sensory anchor pulls the focus away from the distressing material or memories and brings pleasant memories to the forefront where they can be used for support.

Exercise: Finding Sensory Anchors

Choose a memory of something pleasant, preferably of a place or person that gives you a feeling of calm and safety. Do not look for a perfect memory, as that is a misnomer. Negatives can always be associated with (or intrude on) a positive memory. Instead, seek a "good enough" memory. For example, if your grandmother was usually very kind, but a few times lost her temper, restrict your memory to the times (or a time) when she was not angry. If your favorite place in nature is now a housing development, remember it as it was. However, if tragedy is associated with a person or place (violence or disaster), it would be best to pick something or someone else.

Next, awaken the sensory memory (any combination of visual, auditory, tactile, smells, or tastes) associated with that person or place: What do you see and hear in your mind's eye and ear? What is the feeling on your skin? Do you remember any particular smells or tastes? Using the example of a grand-mother, she might be seen in the kitchen with an apron on baking cookies; the associated sound might be her humming as she works; there might be a feeling of warmth on the skin and a related smell of cinnamon or fresh bread; and so on. Once you have elicited one or more sensations, notice what happens elsewhere in your body, particularly in your ANS: What is happening in your heart rate, breathing, body temperature, and level of tension? If for any reason you get an unpleasant reaction (heart pounds, hands or feet get cold, etc.), let that memory go and choose another one. Once you have an image that gives you pleasant body sensations and an increased feeling of calm, you will know this is a potentially useful and safe anchor for you.

To test it, remember a mildly uncomfortable situation (far from the worst) from your work: An irritated client, an incident of feeling inept, a single mild trigger from a client's material. Switch to the calming image of your anchor as soon as your body begins to feel uncomfortable. Bring in as many of the sensory elements as necessary to help your system calm down. Include smells, sounds, changes in temperature, colors, skin sensations, and so on with your image. Enlist all of your senses to flesh it out.

Over time, practicing switching between memories of distressing situations and your sensory anchors will help you to become adept at rapidly turning uncomfortable, stressed body states into calm. Below are two examples of the effective use of sensory anchors. Faith actually discovers her anchor at the source of her distress, and Robert learns to distill the motion of his favorite sport to a small movement he can use even during his work hours.

Accentuate the Positive

Faith is a clinical social worker for children who have cancer. She loves the children and her work, though she peri-

odically succumbs to the stresses of knowing some of them will die. Faith was very clever in her choice of anchor. Her strategy will not be useful to everyone, but it is worth demonstrating. When a strategy like hers works, it is a very valuable adaptation of the technique of sensory anchors.

Faith's major stress was managing her feelings when one of the children died. She usually suffered many days of depression and ruminated on rethinking her career choice. Then she would get irritated with herself and get back on track. Generally, she continued to cope, but it was a little more difficult to bounce back from each subsequent episode. She was becoming fearful of burning out.

With a little help from a consultant, Faith found her strength in the flip side of the source of her depression. For her, the most uplifting events of her life were the periodic (if too few) declarations of a cure. When a child was discharged well and healthy, she celebrated! Elation was the best word she had to describe the feeling. In her body she felt an excited buzz and her lungs expanded so she could take full, deep breaths. Those highs could last several days and "recharge my batteries" to carry on. So, for Faith, her safe place was the same as the source of her stress, her patients, as long as she restricted her focus to the ones who got well.

Together with the consultant, Faith developed a plan: The next time one of the children died, she would mediate her grief with vivid memories of those children who were cured. She would see them, hear their laughter, feel the shared tears of joy. She practiced evoking each of them one at a time. She found that doing this conscientiously helped her to alleviate the depression and questioning when a child died. It was a delicate balance. Faith had to learn how to permit her own grief at the loss, as well as remember the elation of the successes. Over time she was able to find her rhythm in the most trying times.

Subtle Moves

If your sensory anchor is an activity (e.g., dancing), accessing it in times of stress can be particularly powerful but not always practical. Robert's situation demonstrates how an anchor that involves movement can be refined for use anywhere.

> *Robert is a prison counselor in a medium-sized facility. He sees and hears about trauma daily. He describes the whole compound as "vibrating with primordial strain." One of the ways he manages his own stress is by playing handball with friends two days a week. He loves it and knows that his spirits are best on the days he plays.*
>
> *During a period of time when Robert was particularly bothered by job stress, he received help from a local consultant. Together they reviewed—in both image and movement—how Robert feels playing handball. He loved it all, but his favorite play, the one that made him feel most powerful, involved a particular foot position, torso twist, and arm movement. When Robert demonstrated the movement for the consultant, he reported feeling happy, strong, and hopeful.*
>
> *The consultant encouraged Robert to actually rehearse the movement repeatedly, gradually narrowing the range of motion—broad movements becoming smaller and smaller until Robert could feel his favorite play without the consultant seeing any action. Eventually, just the impulses of muscular movement would provoke the positive feelings. This took a bit of practice, but eventually Robert could just imagine the play and feel the movement in his body even though he wasn't actually moving. (If you can, right now, imagine yourself taking a walk. If you can feel a little of the effect without actually moving, you will have the basic idea.) Robert found this to be a powerful tool. On days when he didn't have a game, he could still call up the feeling of it to mediate his stress. A few times he was also able to call up the body memory of playing handball*

when he became overly distressed while working with one of the inmates. With the client none the wiser, Robert could imagine a few handball moves. As he felt the excitement and strength in his body, his hyperarousal drained and he was able to keep his full attention on his client.

The technique used with Robert distills an anchor to its smallest elements, so that it can be used at will, under almost any circumstance. If you have an active anchor, experiment and practice to refine it. This kind of sensory anchor can be very powerful in combating vicarious trauma and other in-session stressors.

How Close Is Too Close?

The term *boundary* is commonly used in psychotherapy jargon to describe several phenomena. Psychotherapists usually think of their professional boundaries as restricted to defining the ethical and sexual limitations of the therapeutic relationship. This section focuses on two additional aspects of boundaries relevant for therapists: those that involve physical distance, or your comfort zone, and those which help you to feel adequately protected inside your own skin, "body armor."

COMFORT ZONE

Your comfort zone is your personal space. Most psychotherapists are familiar with the idea with regard to interpersonal relationships. We often teach our clients about paying attention to distance boundaries, helping them to feel comfortable in interactions with partners, children, coworkers, and friends. But we often neglect our own need for the same during sessions with our clients. Actually, though, boundaries can be vitally important between therapist and client. For the goal of self-care in particular, paying attention to the physical space between therapist and client can be important. Very simple adjustments will aid many practitioners in maintaining a professional distance— a sense of themselves as separate from their clients.

For many of you, taking care of your personal space during therapy sessions will mean having to override what you were told in college or professional training programs. Most psychotherapists are taught to work with clients in close proximity, face-to-face. Actually, sitting closely is not always good for either therapist or client. Recognizing an optimal space between you and a client is usually rather easy, though gaining the knack requires the use of body awareness. You can use the basic skills described earlier in this chapter, noticing your autonomic arousal and other sensations to gauge at which distances you are and are not comfortable. It is important to keep in mind that what is optimal for you will change from day to day, client to client, and session to session. Closeness with a particular client one day does not ensure that closeness will be comfortable the next time (for either of you). Ultimately, finding a distance that is comfortable for both therapist and client is ideal, though that may not always be possible. In those instances, some negotiation and experimentation will help. An example from my own practice may be useful.

My client, Saul, was rather controlling. He liked me to sit within a foot of him and always kept eye contact. Over the first month of sessions, I became more and more uncomfortable sitting so close to him; my shoulders would get tense and I often had a headache by the end of the hour. I found that I was beginning to dread seeing him. Discussing his issues of control did nothing to loosen his need to keep me close. Though he insisted he liked the proximity, I wondered. Sometimes it felt as if there was a cushion of air, like the surface of a clear balloon, pushing at me. That made it hard for me to breathe. At the fourth session, however, I saw something that had evaded me before (sometimes when I am sitting too close, I can't see or think as well as I'd like): Saul's chest was held very high, as if he was holding his breath.

That observation emboldened me to suggest something

different. I asked Saul if it would be OK if I moved my chair back a couple of feet. I promised him I would move back when he wanted me to, but encouraged him to try the experiment. He skeptically agreed. When I moved, he immediately exhaled (as I'd suspected he might). Pointing out what I just observed, I asked, "What happened?" Saul replied that he must have been holding his breath. When I helped him to tune into his breathing, he reported breathing easily. When I asked if I should return to the closer proximity, he just said, "No, that's OK. I'm comfortable with you there." After that session he no longer insisted on us sitting so close, and I became much more comfortable working with him.

Saul was not ready to acknowledge that he had also been uncomfortable with my sitting so close, but the experiment still worked to give us both more "breathing room."

Room to Work

Of course it is an advantage if your office is large. Then you can experiment with furniture placement and greater and smaller distances between seats. But if your office is small, there are still many options.

Rosalyn worked in a family service agency as a psychologist. New to the agency, she was assigned one of the smaller offices, only about 100 square feet: room for a desk, two chairs, and a few books. She often felt that clients were nearly sitting in her lap. It was hard for her to feel any separateness, and sometimes she felt overheated and headachy. The arrangement was also not comfortable for many of her clients; the most fragile ones would startle nearly every time she moved. Inspired by a training course on therapist self-care, Rosalyn took a look at her floor plan. She had originally arranged her desk against the far corner, under the window, to maximize the available floor space. That made it possible for her to sit with her back to the desk, directly opposite her clients, as she had been taught to do. But since she was uncomfortable so much of the time, she decided to experiment with changing things around.

Turning her desk to face the side wall gave Rosalyn more length in the room. That made it possible for her to sit a little further away when she or her client felt the need for more space. Also, her desk had a writing extension that pulled out like a cutting board. When she was feeling most vulnerable, or with the most fragile clients, she pulled the extension out and wrote her notes on it, creating an actual (if narrow) barrier between herself and her client.

That minimal intervention gave Rosalyn and her clients more options for negotiating their proximity in the therapy room. Paying attention to body sensations gave Rosalyn the motivation to experiment and find a more optimal furniture arrangement.

Comfort Zone Exercises

First, if you are unfamiliar with what it feels like in your body to be in proximity (at varying distances) to another, you might practice with a colleague, friend, or family member. You can try a common boundary exercise. You and a partner begin by standing at a distance (10 to 15 feet is preferable). Each of you should take stock of your body sensations for a baseline. Then one of you walks toward the other slowly. Look for the reactions in your body to the changes in distance. Any nuance counts.

Second, beginning with a single client, pay attention to your body sensations, particularly your arousal level, during the session. Experiment with positioning to maintain a comfortable level of arousal in yourself. You can move your chair forward or back. You can also turn your chair so more of your side is turned toward your client, rather than facing head-on. You can write notes or not. If you do write notes, try different styles: write on your lap, on a lap desk or book, at your desk, and so on. The idea is to try many different possibilities so you increase your options. Once you get the idea, you can try the same experiments with as many clients as you like.

Third, look at the floor plan of your office. Is there any way to change the furniture arrangement to your advantage, as Rosalyn did? Feel free to try different arrangements, or to add items that might increase your comfort: a small table, a knickknack or stone, a plant, and so forth.

BODY ARMOR

When dealing with volatile client emotions, feeling a sense of protection on a body level can be a big advantage. Of course, you still want to be able to connect with your client, but sometimes feeling safe and comfortable will make that more possible. For some it is very difficult to grasp the concept that feeling vulnerable does not necessarily increase availability and connection. Sometimes it actually provokes the opposite, withdrawal and restriction. For those of you who will find it beneficial, strategies for increasing body armor follow. (Increasing body armor is a concept I learned in a 4-year professional training course with Bodynamic Institute in Copenhagen, Denmark, 1988–1992.) Use the ANS as a gauge to tell you which interventions are most effective for you, along with the pointers mentioned.

Jill's Vulnerable Chest

> *After 12 years as an incest counselor, Jill was afraid she might need to switch careers, or at least jobs. While in the past she was able to maintain a professional distance in her work, for the last couple of years she has been feeling increasingly affected by the situations and states of her clients. Her agency agreed to pay for outside consultation, hoping to hold onto one of their best therapists.*

Jill: I just can't do it anymore! Their stories didn't used to get to me, but now I am thinking about my clients all the time

and I wake from dreams and nightmares of the scenes they
have described.
Consultant: Is this different than it used to be?
Jill: Yes. For many years I had no difficulties. I didn't take my
clients home with me and they didn't invade my sleep. This
is really getting to me!
Consultant: What do you think changed?

*Because Jill had no problems with her work for many
years, something must now be different. I wanted to see if
we could track it down. If we could identify a trigger, helping her would be easier. But if not, other interventions
were still available.*

Jill: I don't know. I just feel more vulnerable, I guess.
Consultant: Can you identify when you started becoming
more vulnerable to your clients?
Jill: I'm not sure. But certainly I've been more distressed in
the last 2 years or so.

*Was there something relevant in her personal life, either
in the last 2 years or in her past? If so, I might not be able
to help her with the particulars, but could refer her to
someone else for therapy. This kind of supervision can
sometimes get tricky. It is always advisable to maintain a
clear delineation between consultation and therapy. Supervision that crosses that line can contaminate the use-
fulness of the sessions and confuse the relationship between the therapist and the consultant.*

Consultant: Did anything change in your life shortly before
or during that time?
Jill: Nothing of significance. No births, deaths, illnesses,
moves, etc., just more job stress.
Consultant: And what about incest or some similar issue in
your own background?
Jill: No, nothing of the sort. I am sure my distress is not from
my past. I know what it is like to have one of my own issues

triggered by a client issue; that has a different feeling, like anxiety. What I am feeling now is more heavy, depressed, stressed—burdened.

Consultant: Can you tell me how you experience that in your body—both in session and in your daily life?

At the least, identifying the effect on her body could lead us to tools that could give her support, shore her up, so to speak.

Jill: Day to day, like I said: heavy. I feel like I am dragging around. In session I often feel tired and sometimes sad.

Consultant: Imagine being with one of your clients right now, just one. What happens?

Evoking the memory of a typical session might give us some clues to go further with.

Jill: Suddenly I feel very tired.

Consultant: Where?

Jill: All over. I feel like I want to crawl into bed.

Consultant: Is the feeling you have now anything like what you experience during a session?

Jill: Yes, exactly.

Consultant: And when you come back to focus on me and this room?

Jill: Less tired. I feel fairly normal.

Consultant: Then shift your awareness back and forth between the image of your client and the here and now in this room. As you do that, see if you can identify where in your body the tiredness starts from and lifts from. I want to help you find out where, in a way, this client gets to you. Where does he or she get inside you; what is your vulnerable spot?

When there is such a clear difference in response, it can be useful to shuttle awareness between one and the other,

tracking somatic sensations as they change. Jill shifted her
awareness several times before she realized what was hap-
pening.

Jill: [*With a small startle reaction*] That's interesting. My
attention keeps coming to my chest, here [*points to the up-*
per part of the breastbone]. I don't know if that is the answer
to your question, but that's what happened.
Consultant: What happens there as you shift your attention?
Jill: It seems that's where, as you asked, the tiredness starts
and lifts. When I imagine my client, I get tired starting there
[*points to chest*]. Then it sort of radiates out to the rest of
my body. When I bring my attention to this room, that's
where I first start feeling better. So, what does that mean?
Consultant: I don't know yet. First, I'd like to increase your
muscle tone there, help you develop a "thicker skin," so to
speak. Then we can see if that has any impact on how you
are feeling in session and day to day. No guarantees, but I
think it's worth a try. Are you game?
Jill: I guess I'm at the point of being willing to try almost
anything. What should I do?
Consultant: Since it is your chest where you first feel the
tiredness, I'd like to see what happens when you increase
the muscle tone of your chest. Actually, I'll direct you to
increase the tension in the pectoral muscles that cover the
ribs and breastbone. First, try putting the palms of your
hands together at about the height of your chest where
you pointed before. Then push the palms together until
you feel tension under your breasts. That's the pectorals—
you might remember doing a movement like this when you
were a teenager.
Jill: [*Smiling*] Yes, with my girlfriends. We thought it would
increase our bust size.
Consultant: It can do that by increasing the muscle mass underneath the breasts. But that is not my concern. What I am
aiming for is seeing if increasing muscle tone changes anything
for you. Right now the idea is to press your hands together and

hold the tension until the chest muscles just begin to feel tired and then release very, very slowly. That way you can gradually build up tone. You can use push-ups for a similar effect. Go ahead and do that three times with a rest between each. [*Jill slowly tenses and releases three times.*] What do you feel?

Jill: I feel a bit stronger there. Maybe my mood lifted slightly, but I'm not sure.

Consultant: That's fine. Next I want you to imagine being with that same client again. Notice what happens, how you feel, and if there is any difference, positive or negative.

> *It is extremely important when evaluating any exercise to be completely open to either positive or negative results. Especially when working with muscle tone, the result is unpredictable.*

Jill: Well, I didn't get that same jolt of tiredness. I'm curious to see if it changes anything with an actual client. But how can I do that tensing in an actual session?

Consultant: First, it may be most useful to be increasing the muscle tone there on a regular basis. That can thicken your skin. To do that, you can use the exercise we tried here or push-ups. Just remember to ease off at the beginning of tiredness in the muscles. If you exhaust them, you may lose the protective potential. For use in the session, let's design a technique for you. Try pushing your palms together again and see if you can isolate where you feel the tension build in your chest. [*Jill uses her thumbs to point to a spot just about halfway between her waist and her collarbone.*] Then release that slowly. Now place your arms in a more normal in-session position. [*Jill's hands meet in her lap.*] From that position, see if you can make tension in the same spot.

Jill: I can't do it if my arms stay relaxed. But if I press the heels of my hands together slightly, then I can feel it.

Consultant: So keep trying it, gradually decreasing the observable movement.

Jill: I think I am doing that. Can you see it?

Consultant: Yes, but only because I am looking carefully and know what to look for. I doubt most clients would notice—maybe one who is an athlete or personal trainer, but not others. You could try it a few times during a session. Maybe add a mental note like, "I am keeping my client's feelings out of my chest." Something like that. What would fit?

Jill: Perhaps, "If I don't let this client get to me, I'll be better able to help her."

Consultant: Fine. You might write that down so you remember it. Try both the tensing movement and that phrase for the next 2 weeks. Pay attention to how you feel before, during, and after sessions and at the end of the day. Feel free to edit your mental phrase if you find something better. I'll also be interested to hear what happens with your dreams. Don't worry if this doesn't help, as there are more strategies to try. It is important to evaluate honestly so I'll know where to help you next time. Keeping a log would be useful so we can see any visible patterns.

Jill returned to the consultant 2 weeks later much encouraged. She still had a few client dreams, but no nightmares. Her day-to-day energy and mood were much improved. The increased muscle tone appeared to be working to give Jill a more protective, thicker skin over her chest. Encouraged, the consultant recommended that Jill also get into a regular exercise program, something she used to do and had stopped—curiously enough—about 2 years before. Over the next couple of months, as Jill became more physically fit, she also became more fit to continue her very demanding job.

There is no way to really know, but it is possible that the timing of the onset of Jill's symptoms and her reduction in exercise may be linked. Nonetheless, it now seems clear that increasing muscle tone and adding regular exercise were important skills for Jill's self-care repertoire.

Exercise: Thickening Your Skin

Having a thick skin is always useful for reducing feelings of vulnerability and permeability. If you feel like your clients are getting to you in ways that are not healthy for you—or helpful for them—then thickening your skin might be called for.

Start with one client who seems to intrude on you in a way that you do not like. Imagine that he or she is in front of you with the same distance and positioning that you usually have in person. Pay attention to your body as you imagine being with this client. If you cannot get a sense of the client through your memory, you can try this first step when you are actually with the client. But then follow the next steps by yourself (or with a colleague or supervisor).

Notice where in your body you feel vulnerable to this client. Where does this client or his material get to you, or get under your skin? Is it in your chest? Your arms? Your stomach? Your forehead? Your groin? Somewhere else?

In the place where you feel vulnerable, tense up the muscles that cover that area. For example, if the vulnerability is in your stomach, you can tense up stomach muscles by doing a sit-up or partial sit-up—on the floor or in a chair. Just bring your head and knees a little closer in a crunch if you are lying down, or raise your feet slightly off the floor if you are sitting in a chair. You can also try to suck in your gut. You will know you are being effective when you feel the muscles across your belly tense up. For vulnerability in the back, you can try pulling your shoulder blades together or standing with your back to a wall and pushing your elbows into the wall. For the forehead, furrow or raise your eyebrows. To increase tension in the groin, you can raise or tighten the pelvic floor. The commonly used Kegel exercises are good for this purpose. If you cannot find the right way to tense up in your spot of vulnerability, feel free to send me a brief e-mail (babette@trauma.cc). Mention that you are reading this book and name the area where you would like to feel a thicker skin. I will be happy to suggest how you can achieve that.

Once you find the correct spot and tensing movement, hold the tension only until the muscles begin to be tired, and then release the tension very slowly. That will leave a little tension when you are done.

Next, imagine being with your client again and see if there is any difference: Do you feel worse, better, the same? If you feel less vulnerable when you imagine the client, then you might work to distill the tensing movement down to a small one you can do actively in the session (as the consultant helped Jill). For stomach tensing, you cannot drop to the floor to do a sit-up in the middle of a session. So you would want to try to get some of that same tension while sitting still in your chair. To distill a movement for increasing stomach tension, for example, you could raise your thighs slightly, together or one at a time. This requires stomach muscles, and the movement can be nearly imperceptible to an observer. In addition or alternatively, you can do the same tensing as a muscle-toning exercise on a regular basis and see if that helps increase your feeling of thickened skin with that client. Remember that this is an experiment and you may need to try several exercises or body areas before one works for you. Do not worry, though, if this exercise is not effective for you, as there are more to try.

Fashion and Bling Bling

How you dress can enhance or diminish your feeling of separation or boundary with your client. You may already be paying attention to how you dress with clients, either consciously or instinctively. Which items in your wardrobe give you a greater feeling of security or stability? Are there certain clothes you wear on days when you feel more fragile or on days when you feel more masterful? Are you dressing in a particular fashion with certain clients? In general, paying attention to your workday attire can be used to advantage in taking better care of yourself.

In particular, it can be a useful strategy to designate an item of clothing (one you already have, or one you purchase) as a "bulletproof vest." You can wear this particular item on days when you feel particularly vulnerable, or with the clients who get to you most easily.

Sometimes items of jewelry can also serve this purpose. Remember Wonder Woman? She had bracelets that deflected bullets and such. In a similar vein, you can imbue your own medallions or bracelets with "protective power" to deflect feelings that are not yours. After reading this, you may even now realize that you wear a particular pendant because it exactly covers a particularly vulnerable spot or makes you feel strong. If not, find one that will.

Stephanie is an experienced psychologist. In the past year she changed jobs and is now working for an eating disorders clinic. She has sought consultation because she is already on the verge of burnout. She often feels exhausted and edgy and complains that she is constantly hungry— previously not a usual state for her. Stephanie is fairly confident that this is the result of projective identification, that her clients are projecting their exhaustion and hunger into her. She wants to learn how to get them to stop.

The following consultation excerpt begins about 15 minutes into the session. We had already discussed a couple of Stephanie's clients as well as her understanding of projective identification. I suggested that she may not need to get her clients to change for her to feel better, that she may be able to bar their access to her system. At this point

she was skeptical but interested. In my own mind, I was al-
ready speculating where the difficulty might stem from.
Sometimes it is multiple sources, sometimes a single major
one. I had several things in mind to explore with her. Spa-
tial boundaries were the first on my list.

Consultant: Tell me about how you and your clients typically sit together.

Stephanie: To some extent, it depends on the client. Usually
I sit in a chair and my client sits on a couch.

Consultant: What kind of distance is between you?

Stephanie: Typically we're rather close, our knees a foot or
so apart. Most of my clients are hungry for contact as well
as for food.

Consultant: So how is it for you to sit so closely?

Stephanie: To be honest, it took some getting used to. On
my previous job—an HMO—I had a much bigger office; I
was used to 3 or so feet between.

Consultant: What took getting used to?

Stephanie: The feeling of being crowded. But I've adjusted
and seem to manage from session to session.

Consultant: Would it be OK to experiment here and see
what happens in you if we were to sit that close? [*Currently
we are sitting across the distance of my consultation room,
about 5 feet from each other.*]

Stephanie: OK. Already I feel a little nervous, but that is
probably just performance anxiety.

Consultant: You are probably right, but it could be something else or a combination. Let's pay attention to your initial
response before we move at all. How do you experience that
nervousness?

Stephanie: What do you mean?

Consultant: What are the sensations in your body that are
signals to you that you are nervous? Are you shaking? Cold?
Feeling your heart beat fast?

Stephanie: None of those. It's more like mild butterflies in my stomach.

> *Based on that report and my own observation, I summarized that her sympathetic nervous system was not very activated, so her arousal level was low. But I wanted to take care when we sat closer. This was consultation, not therapy, and I didn't want to provoke an unhelpful response.*

Consultant: So would it be OK to try to sit closer?
Stephanie: Yes. Now I'm curious.
Consultant: So, you decide: Which of us do you want to move?
Stephanie: I think I will.
Consultant: Then you move closer a bit—not the full distance. I want you to pay attention to what happens to those butterflies, and any other sensations you notice in your body. [*She moves forward about a foot and a half.*] What happens?
Stephanie: Nothing in particular. I feel the same. Can I move closer now? [*I nod. She moves forward an additional foot.*] Now something changes. I feel a little tense and I'm starting to get a headache.

> *As I had a mild headache myself, I wanted to see if we could determine if she was picking up on mine, if I was picking up on hers, or if it was just a coincidence that we both had slightly achy heads.*

Consultant: Where do you feel the headache? [*She identifies the exact location of my headache.*] This may surprise you, but you have perfectly described the headache I came in with today. Are you generally prone to feel what others feel?
Stephanie: Do you think this has a bearing on my exhaustion?
Consultant: It may, and also on your hunger. It is difficult for many people to distinguish their own from another's feelings, and even sensations, when in very close proximity—

think of the couples you've worked with who can't maintain separate feelings.

Stephanie: Well, it is true that I often tune into my children and husband. My kids know they can't fake a stomachache to get out of school because I can tell when it's not true. All I have to do is give them a hug. But if you are right, why should my clients' hunger or exhaustion continue to dog me between sessions? That doesn't happen with my children's ills or hurts.

Consultant: It sounds like you are very aware of your intuition with your children; you know that you can feel their pain. Awareness can make a big difference. You can certainly try that with your clients. Just being aware of the possibility that you are tuning in to their hunger and tiredness may be enough to free you between sessions. However, if that is not adequate, you may need to change your seating arrangement.

Stephanie: But I can't change the physical distance with my clients; my supervisor insists they need the closeness. What else can I do?

This was tricky. As an outside consultant, I had to be careful. It would not help Stephanie for me to put her in conflict with the policies of her workplace, no matter how strong my opinions.

Consultant: I'm thinking of a couple of things. First of all, you may want to talk with your supervisor about working with boundaries for the benefit of your clients. That is certainly an issue for most (if not all) of those with eating disorders. If you are having discomfort sitting that close, there is a good chance your clients may be too. The only way to know is to experiment and ask. Helping clients to find the balance between comfortable boundaries and comfortable closeness can be fruitful work. However, if your supervisor won't budge, then there are clandestine ways you can increase the boundary for yourself, even sitting a foot away.

Stephanie: Well, I want to leave here feeling hopeful, like I have a couple of things I can actually do to take care of myself even if nothing changes at work. I like the idea of increasing my awareness; it would be neat if that did the trick. And it would be good to also have a concrete tool to use if being mindful is not enough. I like the idea of clandestine boundaries. Does that mean I could increase distance from my client without anyone catching on?

Consultant: It has that potential anyway. Remember, this is just an experiment. That means I want you to try one thing for a day or two, at most a week, and evaluate how it affects you, both for better and for worse. That way you can find which, if any, strategies really work for you.

Stephanie: OK. I'll make notations after each session.

Consultant: Yes, and at the end of each day. You might keep a separate journal for this, so that you can keep your experiments private. How do you usually feel when you leave work, and in the evening?

Stephanie: Exhausted and ravenous. That's where we started.

Consultant: Good. That gives us a great gauge to use. Measure each evening on a scale of 1 to 10 your level of exhaustion, 10 being the worst. Looking back, can you guesstimate your average?

Stephanie: Certainly some days have been 10s. But probably I average around 7. So, what can I do if I can't move my chair and awareness is not enough?

Consultant: In general, have you ever noticed feeling differently, depending on how you dress?

Stephanie: Well, on weekends, I usually wear jeans and sometimes call them my "tough" clothes. Is that what you mean?

Consultant: Do you feel differently in them?

Stephanie: Sure, a bit more masculine, less vulnerable than when I wear a dress or thin slacks and light sweaters.

Consultant: With your clients, you can use the same idea. Think about your wardrobe, what you usually wear to work. Are there any outfits or items that you could put on to feel more thickness—space or distance—between you and your clients?

Stephanie: Since it's winter, I could try a bulky sweater. I also have a leather vest that I like; it's soft, but thicker than cloth. I could try those.

Consultant: Sounds like they have good potential. What about jewelry? Do you remember Wonder Woman?

Stephanie: [*laughing*] You mean like her deflector bracelets? Could I deflect the projective identifications?

Consultant: [*laughing, too*] Exactly! Of course your bracelets wouldn't have that actual power. You have to imagine that they do. Anyway, I think you have enough things to try in the next 2 weeks.

> When Stephanie returned 2 weeks later for her next consultation, she reported that several things had worked. First, her increased awareness that her clients might be getting to her on a body level had made her more alert. That simple insight managed to reduce her hunger following sessions. She continued to feel hungry during the session but afterward was able to let it go. However, awareness alone was not enough to protect her from exhaustion. She experimented with clothing and found that her bulky sweater worked particularly well. On the three days she'd worn it, she rated her tiredness level as only 3. The leather vest did not work at all. She was still intrigued by the idea of deflectors, and we explored what pendant she might have or buy to use for that purpose. All in all, most significant for Stephanie was the discovery that she could do something concrete to disrupt a projective identification, as she continued to call it. She no longer felt it to be inevitable nor so powerful, now that she had some tools to intervene.

Pushing Away With the Eyes

Some people are particularly vulnerable during eye contact with others. Those with soft, open, and inviting eyes are the most likely to engender openness and trust. As those traits figure strongly in the qualities that attract clients to us, many therapists fall into this category. However, sometimes that kind of openness in the eyes can also make the boundary between therapist and client foggy. When that happens, the therapist can take in too much or feel too exposed. If these concepts feel personally familiar to you, it might be of use for you to learn how to have more choice about eye contact with your clients. You can also learn to have more control over how eye contact affects you, and the impact on you of what you actually see.

Most simply, Hodges and Wegner (1997) reminded us that the mere action of averting your gaze—even for a few seconds—from emotionally expressive clients can often be enough to help you better regulate your own responses. Such a commonsensical proposal becomes even more useful with the added understanding of mirror neurons (see Chapter 2). For these to activate, an action must be seen. That is why "when we carefully attend to others performing a series of manual activities, we find our own muscles 'helping them out'" (Hatfield et al., 1994, p. 32).

Pushing away with your eyes is another way to manage unpleasant responses to eye contact. In learning this skill, as with the others offered in this book, it is not meant that you should change your normal way of looking at people or being in visual contact at all times. This skill is meant to add an additional tool to your repertoire, to use or not use as appropriate. Experiment with it first. If it is useful to you, add it to your toolkit.

Body psychotherapists trained in the theories of Wilhelm Reich call this idea of pushing away with the eyes creating an *ocular defense*. It is meant to enhance your sense of distance between you and your client, to create a boundary or separation between your own and your client's eyes. It can be helpful, particularly when increased separation would feel protective or calming for you. It can also be indicated when it would give you a better feeling of professional distance for helping your client.

It is best to practice this skill with another person (partner, colleague, friend, etc.). In the absence of such assistance, you can try it with an animal (cats work well). First, though, it may be good to try it looking in the mirror at yourself:

1. Tune into body awareness, particularly around your eyes and face. However, also notice other aspects of your body per previous instructions (see Chapter 2), including sensations in your gut.
2. Then notice how your eyes and the area around them look. Soft, hard, inviting, rejecting, smooth, wrinkled?
3. Next, tense up the muscles of and around your eyes, so that they look less inviting when you look at yourself, and they feel harder on a physical level, more defended. If you do it correctly, you will feel tension in and around your eyes, and the scope of your vision will narrow and may become sharper.
4. Take it easy at first so that you do not give yourself a headache. If you do, just ease off and it will subside.
5. Practice shifting between relaxing your eyes and tensing them.
6. Gradually, reduce the tension *around* your eyes while maintaining the tension of your eyes themselves. Using the mirror will help with this. The goal is to be able to maintain maximum eye tension without that tension being easily observed.
7. When you develop some confidence, you can try it with a family member (children are great because they are often sensitive to nuances of expression). You can also try it on the street or in a store.
8. Experiment with changing your eye tension and see if that affects how people treat you and approach or avoid you in public.
9. Once you gain some confidence, take your new skill

into your office. When a client begins to talk about something that distresses you, try tensing your eyes and pushing away. You may want to add a mental note, something like, "It is OK to not take in my client's distress." Find your own words that best suit your own situation.

10. Notice how you feel, including your level of arousal, before and after you apply the method.

As a side note, you can apply the same strategy if unwanted strangers often approach you on the street. Hardening the eyes can change an inadvertent message of invitation to a purposeful rebuff.

Keeping Your Edges

Your skin is your most obvious and concrete boundary: your edge. It is the material that holds all of you in, and holds everything and everyone else out. Solid as the skin is, though, it is something that is easy to lose contact with. When a sense of the body's edge is lost, separation between the self and another may become more difficult. Good skin awareness can help you stay in optimal self-contact and aid in differentiating your own states from those of your client.

During a session, the easiest way to get a sense of your body edges is to feel your skin inside your clothes. You can try one or more of these:

- Move your feet a little inside your shoes and feel the insole of the shoe against the skin of the bottom of your foot. If you are wearing socks or stockings, you may want to feel the material against your foot. What sensations are you aware of? What kind of inner surfaces are you contacting? Rough, smooth, soft, scratchy, or something else?
- Slightly shift your weight in your chair so that you can feel the seat of the chair against your buttocks. Again, you might want to focus on the seat or on your

clothes—whatever works best for you.

- Feel your legs inside your trousers or skirt. Slight movement will help to slide the material against your skin and will help you to feel that edge more clearly.
- For areas that are unclothed, such as your hands and face, you can achieve the same effect by focusing on the difference between your skin temperature and the air temperature. Of course, if the temperatures are quite close, that might not be so easy. You can also rub your hands together or rub your hand on your arm and feel the friction of each against the other.
- Between sessions, splashing cool water on your hands and arms or on your face will help to highlight those edges.

If feeling your edges is difficult for you, training this awareness when you are not with a client might be helpful. When you take a bath or shower, use a slightly rough cloth or sponge or a cool spray of water to help you feel your skin—only do this if it is comfortable for you. You can use your awareness of your autonomic arousal to gauge if this is useful for you or not. If you become nervous or dissociated doing these or any other exercises, stop and use others that calm you down.

Controlling Empathic Imagery

Imagining the stories we hear from clients can boost empathy with them. However, it can also cause problems. Visualizing the distressing and traumatic events of others puts us into the position of eyewitness—one of the categories in the *DSM-IV* that qualifies for PTSD. Moreover, many who habitually imagine client stories (consciously or unconsciously) do so in the first person, as if it was happening to them (Maxfield, 1997). Obviously this is not a problem for some therapists. But if it is a problem for you, some simple, commonsense interventions will help to put you in charge of your imagery.

Following his graduate studies, Bob worked at his local Department of Veterans Affairs, first as an intern and later as a staff psychologist. He had never been in the armed services himself, but he enjoyed the opportunity to provide service to the VA. However, when he married and began his family, he felt the need to earn more money and left the VA to go into general private practice. That did not end his ties to the military, though. Yearly he received several referrals, from the VA and privately, of military personnel—enlisted and officers, those actively serving as well as veterans.

During the first 8 years of his therapist life, Bob heard many accounts of the kinds of horrors that military men and women face during war and peacetime. He thought he managed well. During the 2001–2002 war in Afghanistan, though, he began to "work overtime." He often found himself thinking excessively about his military clients during his free time. He also became edgy and developed sleeping difficulties, sometimes waking from nightmares of war.

Bob struggled a long time, trying to figure out why his clients' stories were getting to him now. One evening, while watching the news, he had an epiphany: The pictures he saw of the Afghan war were similar to the ones he was seeing in his dreams with his clients' faces. The next day he realized that as he was listening to one client's experiences, he was picturing them in his mind's eye, using film clips from the news as his template.

A sense of control—mastery over one's world and mind— is essential for minimizing the negative risks of helping distressed people. Being in charge of the imagery in your own mind is a major step in that direction. A few simple interventions can give any therapist a secure sense of control over what are often judged to be uncontrollable intrusions.

TO PICTURE OR NOT TO PICTURE

This illustration typifies how a common practice that aims to enhance therapist performance can actually detract from it.

Therkild was a counselor for a Holocaust project. As part of his job, he conducted sessions with Holocaust survivors, detailing their experiences and helping them make sense of their lives. The stories he heard were, of course, horrific. Therkild believed that this project was highly significant, and he was proud to participate. However, he regularly suffered as a result. Though he wanted to continue with this work, he was having increasing trouble sleeping and bouts of severe agitation (hyperarousal)—typical symptoms of vicarious traumatization. Moreover, he was becoming hopeless about the future—a common symptom of burnout. He knew the source of his difficulties but did not want to quit. On the advice of a friend, he sought consultation.

With help, Therkild was able to zero in on his vulnerable points. Among other issues, the consultant identified Therkild's habit of visualizing the stories he was being told as a possible source of his difficulties. Therkild felt it was his duty to try to imagine what his clients had experienced. He would consciously visualize during sessions, trying to see the details of the horrific events the client had gone through; he hoped it would make him a more sensitive counselor. Unfortunately, however, the images he conjured during the interview sessions continued to appear unbidden at other times, often in his dreams. He was not able to shake the pictures or the feelings they stirred in him.

The consultant suggested Therkild might examine whether his habit of visualization actually enhanced his abilities as a counselor. They discussed the common assumption that sharing the other's experience would always be helpful. It was the consultant's notion that this was not necessarily the case, that this practice could actually hamper Therkild's ability. At the least, he was suffering because of it. The only way to know if visualization was the key to his vicarious trauma was to make an experiment: try it both ways, alternating from session to session. He was instructed to pay attention to his body awareness and emotions before and after each session. Only then would he be able to determine what was best for him.

They agreed that for the next week, Therkild would keep his visual focus in the room for some sessions and continue to visualize for others. He would keep a log of what happened from session to session. Ahead of time, they discussed strategies to help keep Therkild alert in the here and now if he found himself falling into habitual visualizations. The consultant suggested that paying closer attention to the client's words and gestures, and periodically looking around the room, would be helpful in keeping Therkild focused. During the sessions, Therkild listened to his clients as always and asked appropriate questions. For half of the sessions he was mostly able to refrain from making pictures in his mind, relying on the strategies he and his consultant had come up with.

Though he felt a bit awkward in restricting himself, Therkild noticed a difference immediately. He did not become nearly as anxious as usual during sessions where he was not visualizing, and he was much calmer after those sessions. He had no doubts that what was described had been horrific. He felt very sympathetic. But without visualizing alongside them, he was not suffering with those clients. On the first night of his experiment he slept more peacefully than he would have expected. Moreover, in reflecting back, he judged that the sessions where he had kept from visualizing had gone at least as well as usual. During those sessions, he had actually remembered a couple of important questions that he often forgot.

After a week of experimentation, Therkild weighed the pros and cons of visualizing his client's stories, He concluded that, for the most part, he would permanently change his habit and stop requiring himself to see the stories. He knew he could still use that tool if material came up that he could not otherwise understand. But generally he wanted to relieve himself of that added stressor.

This simple change was rather easy for Therkild to apply because, for the most part, his habit of visualization had usually been voluntary; he had chosen to create imagery. This is not always the case. Some therapists find themselves visualizing the circumstances of clients reflexively. Halting an unconscious habit is a little more involved, as the case of Tina shows below.

CONTROLLING UNINVITED IMAGES

This example involves techniques inspired by neurolinguistic programming's concept of *submodalities* (Andreas & Andreas, 1987; Bandler, 1985). The idea is simple. A submodality is a feature or characteristic of an image. For example, volume is one submodality of sound, clarity is another. Submodalities for visual images include size, shape, color, distance, and so on. The goal is to take control of any visual or auditory images that are invoked when hearing (or thinking about) distressing stories or reports. By changing elements of the images (the submodalities), they can be better managed.

> *Tina had been a therapist in a rape crisis center for about a year when she realized her lifestyle was becoming more and more restricted. Though she had never suffered physical violence, she was finding herself behaving and feeling in ways similar to many of her clients. Of course, like most who work with victims of violence, Tina had become more aware of danger and more cautious. But in the last couple of months, what had been sensible caution had crossed the line to become debilitating limitations. She decided she needed counseling and engaged a psychotherapist.*
>
> *Tina told her new therapist that she was behaving more and more like a woman who had been raped and that scared her very much. She had also had a few anxiety attacks (racing heart, cold sweat, disorientation) while out at night and was becoming more and more concerned The therapist helped Tina understand the concept of vicarious*

traumatization and suggested they find out what her spe-
cial vulnerabilites were. Among other things, the thera-
pist focused closely on how Tina processed the information
she was given by her clients, particularly how she heard
their experiences of rape.

"Oh, I don't just hear it," Tina replied. "I see it." Upon
close scrutiny, the therapist learned that images of the
client's rape automatically appeared in Tina's mind's eye.
She never planned to visualize the rapes. "It just happens."
Actually, it was the one aspect of her job that she hated.
Tina loved helping the women (and the occasional man),
but she dreaded the images that would then fill her head.
The psychotherapist believed there was an additional com-
pounding factor. It was Tina's tendency to visualize her
client's rape in the first person, as if it was happening to
her, rather than to the client.

This is a common occurrence with visualization (Maxfield, 1997). While first-person imagery can be useful in learning a new skill or sport, it actually can compound the therapist's risk for vicarious traumatization. Of course it is a good idea to control imagery that is obviously distressing to you—during a session, immediately following a session, or between sessions with your client. If in doubt, being mindful and taking stock of your arousal level during sessions and when a client leaves can be helpful. As we will see in the examples below, it is common for psychotherapists to believe that visualizing client stories enhances empathy. Actually, that is probably correct. But at what cost? Is visualization necessary to empathy? Probably the answer varies from practitioner to practitioner, and perhaps also from client to client. There is always a fine line to walk: maximizing useful empathy without endangering the mental health of the practitioner. For each of you the balance will be slightly different, an individual matter for you to negotiate for yourself (or with the help of a consultant or your own therapist). Below are several exercises that will help those readers with this tendency. First, back to Tina.

Tina's therapist suggested that Tina could gain control of the images in her mind's eye. Tina was a bit dubious but was willing to try anything to feel better and be able to continue in her job. They did not jump directly to working with the debilitating, frightening images. Initially, they worked with neutral and positive images. The therapist first had Tina visualize a blue ball 12 inches in diameter floating in front of her chest, 3 feet away. Then the therapist instructed Tina to change aspects of the visualization—different color, distance, size, shape, and so on— changing one submodality at a time. When Tina became confident in her ability, the therapist gave more complicated instructions. Finding that she was able to manipulate these simple images boosted Tina's confidence.

At this point it is relevant to mention that had Tina's (or Therkild's, for that matter) images been of an auditory or tactile nature, the same interventions could be used, changing the instructions to focus on sounds or skin sensations instead of visual images. The effect can be the same, though the adaptation of the instructions might be a bit more challenging. Sometimes the images are not actually seen but are sensed or felt. In those instances, the instructions can also be adapted. For example, a consultant could say, "Sense a 12-inch blue ball in front of you. Feel it shrink in size," and so forth.

At the next session, they continued to train Tina's sense of control. The therapist suggested that Tina choose a nontraumatic activity she had observed. As she liked to watch the Wimbledon tennis championship, she chose that. It was a plus for the purposes of the exercise that Tina did not actually play tennis. That way she could experiment with altering her first-person image with an activity her body did not actually recognize, just as she would eventually do with altering her imagination of a rape that she had (thankfully) also not experienced.

The therapist instructed Tina to start with one view—

that of the player or that of the observer—and periodically switch her perspective. First she would imagine playing the game, how the swing of the racket would feel, or moving on her feet. Then she would change and imagine observing someone else playing the game as she did while watching television. The idea was for Tina to have the experience of controlling the imagery, without the stress of upsetting content. Once she became skilled at controlling images in this way, she could graduate to controlling the images that had been plaguing her.

This entire process took several weeks. Applying it in her working situation was gradual. At first Tina practiced being an observer, rather than a participant, in her mind's eye. Eventually, she learned that she could visualize other things when hearing the stories of rape. Like Therkild, Tina found that she did not have to picture the violence to be sensitive and empathetic to what her client had experienced.

EXERCISES FOR IMAGERY CONTROL

If you think you could benefit from imagery control strategies in your own work, here are three exercises you can try. Remember, if you are not someone who has visual images, you can try the same procedure with the kinds of images you do have: auditory, tactile, body position and movement, and so forth.

Imagery Control Exercise 1

In your mind's eye, imagine an everyday object. It does not matter what it is, so long as it is not associated with stress. If you are not able to visualize, do not worry. Many people do not visualize. You are welcome to alter the exercise, exchanging *feel* or *sense* for *see* or *visualize*. Exercise 2 involves auditory images. As Tina did, manipulate your images (visual, sensory—whatever) of the object in as many ways (submodalities) as you can think of. One at a time, change its size, distance, color, shape, and so on.

Imagery Control Exercise 2

Imagine that you have a tape recorder beside you with a good selection of controls for altering the submodalities of volume, speed, pitch, direction, and so on.

Choose something neutral or pleasant to start with: a song, dialogue from television, a story read aloud, or some such. Then play around with altering its features. Make it louder or softer. Raise and lower the pitch. Play it backwards, play it forwards. Try changing the speed. You can also change the voice to another speaker—e.g., John Wayne, Donald Duck, Madonna—any voice you like.

Next you can try the same tools with a sound or voice that has some emotional meaning for you. Just make sure to gradually increase the difficulty or emotional charge of the sound you are working with. Do not go to the next level of challenge until you have mastered the current level.

This is also a great technique for those who are plagued by critical voices in their heads. Just change the critical voice to Elmo or Mickey Mouse and see if the criticism has the same sting.

It is equally useful for, say, the abuse therapist who cannot get the sound of crying children out of his head, or the veterans' counselor who keeps hearing gunfire. Learning to take command of the audio controls can help these distressing sounds and others that are replayed in your mind to diminish or even disappear.

Imagery Control Exercise 3

Practice watching a pleasant or neutral image on an imagined television monitor. Assume you have a full set of controls for making the picture larger or smaller, changing the focus, changing the direction, altering the speed, changing the color palette, moving the television closer or farther from you, turning the sound up and down, or turning the picture on and off. One at a time, experiment with changing as many of the features (submodalities) as you can.

Once you become adept, you can try images that have more emotional meaning for you. Just make sure to take your time and gradually increase the difficulty of the images. Do not move on to something more potentially upsetting before you have mastered control of a less stressful image.

Eventually, you can try the same thing with images from your work that plague you. When you find yourself imagining something horrible that you are being told about, move the screen farther away, blur the image, step out of first person and become the observer, look at something else, or turn off the image altogether and just listen to your client.

The idea is to reinforce for yourself that *you have full control* of whether and how much you will try on or witness the experiences of your clients.

Chapter 4

Thinking Clearly

The Neurophysiology of Clear Thinking is the feature theory section of this chapter. Following that, skill building sections to help the therapist to "know thyself," strengthen the observer, and control self-talk, and bolster the internal frameworks that aid clear thinking. Additional sections on nurturing your work space and structured self-care will guide the strengthening of external, environmental, frameworks that can enhance clear thinking.

THEORY
The Neurophysiology of Clear Thinking

Most of us have difficulty thinking clearly when we are agitated or highly stressed. There is good reason for this. The explanation is found in understanding how the brain and body function under stress. The key to maintaining clear thinking is to keep calm—even when challenged to the maximum by a demanding client or boss. This chapter builds on the theory and tools from previous chapters.

Now, in the 21st century, it is easy to think that brain study is an old science. In fact, however, it is still in its infancy. Only a few years ago, Richard Restak (1995) remarked that the majority of knowledge about the brain had been accumulated only in the past few years. As with the development of any branch of science, hypotheses come and go. However, in each area, there are always some theories that continue to hold up under scrutiny. One of the most useful, especially for the purposes of this chapter, is Paul MacLean's (1973) mid-20th-century concept of the *triune brain*.

According to MacLean's now widely accepted schema, the human brain consists of three regions or levels. Each has its own specific areas of control and responsibility though all are, of course, connected. The lowest level, the *reptilian brain*, is the region that comprises the brainstem and cerebellum. In the main, the reptilian brain preserves body function and basic life support, including stabilizing temperature and respiration. It is neither rational nor emotional; it just continues to do its essential job. Even when there is a total loss of cortical function, the brainstem functions on.

MacLean named the middle brain region the *limbic system*, a term commonly used today. It includes the thalamus, hypothalamus, amygdala, and hippocampus. As the old medical school joke goes, the limbic system is responsible for the "four Fs of survival": fight, flight, feeding, and sexual reproduction. The limbic system is known to be the emotional center of the brain. It furthers survival of the individual and of the species by provoking body systems into action to avoid danger and pain, and to seek safety and pleasure.

With regard to evolution, the neocortex is the most recently developed of the brain's regions. Its higher functions are what separate the primates, particularly humans, from animals lower on the evolutionary scale. The neocortex takes survival in humans to a higher level. For example, the ability to construct shelters where they are advantageous, rather than having to seek shelter only where nature provides it (e.g., a cave), is one of the evolutionary steps-up facilitated by the neocortex. The neocortex also makes planning, judgment, and rational thought possible. Creativity, art, music, and such are the result of the interplay between cortical and limbic regions.

Germane to this chapter, a balance between the functions of the neocortex and the limbic system is necessary for therapists to be able to maintain clear thinking despite work pressures and client distress.

AUTOMATIC RESPONSE VERSUS RATIONAL THINKING

There is an ongoing disagreement in psychology as to which comes first, thought or feeling. Those with a cognitive-behavioral bent see thought as the precursor (Wolpe, 1969). And we all know our thoughts do, at least sometimes, affect our feelings. On the other side are those with a more emotional or body-oriented influence who believe that feeling preceeds thought. The argument dates at least from the late 1800s when followers of James (1884) and Cannon (1929) argued for their views. Joseph LeDoux (1996) has an excellent discussion of those arguments in *The Emotional Brain*. The truth probably is somewhere in-between, sometimes thought is the precursor, sometimes feeling is. The focus here illuminates Cannon's view (as well as Damasio's, as discussed earlier) by looking to the body for the underlying source of feeling: the sensory nervous system and the limbic system structure, the amygdala.

The Early Warning System

The amygdala acts as a kind of early warning system. It processes emotion before feelings become consciousness in the cortex. Smiling when hearing the voice of someone you love before you have had any thoughts is an example of the amygdala's communication speed. It works like this (you may want to refer back to the CNS chart featured in Figure 2.1): The sound of the loved one's voice is communicated to the amygdala via exteroceptive auditory nerves in the sensory nervous system. The amygdala then generates an emotional response to that information (likely pleasure or happiness in this example) by releasing hormones that stimulate the visceral muscles of the autonomic nervous system and which can be felt as pleasant sensations in the stomach and elsewhere. Last, the amygdala sets in motion an accompanying somatic nervous system (skeletal muscle) response, in this case, tensing muscles at the sides of the mouth into a smile.

A similar process occurs with other types of stimuli, including trauma. When someone is threatened, the amygdala perceives danger through the exteroceptive senses (sight, hearing, touch, taste, and smell) and sets in motion the series of hormone releases and other somatic reactions that quickly lead to the defensive responses of fight, flight, or freeze. Epinephrine arouses the sympathetic nervous system, stopping digestive processes (hence dry mouth). At the same time, it raises heart rate and respiration to quickly increase oxygenation in the muscles to meet the demands of self-defense (for a review of ANS function, see Chapter 3).

The amygdala is immune to the effect of stress hormones and may even continue to sound an alarm inappropriately. That could be said to be the core of PTSD—the amygdala continuing an alarm even after the actual danger has ceased. Unimpeded, the amygdala stimulates the same hormonal release as during actual threat, leading to the same responses: preparation for (or actual) fight, flight, or freeze. The war veteran who dives for cover at the sound of a car backfiring is an example of the amygdala's power to re-provoke the body's emergency response in the absence of actual danger.

Why does the amygdala continue to perceive danger when there is none? For the purposes of therapist self-care, how could the activity of the amygdala impede a therapist's clear thinking?

The Rational System

The hippocampus helps to process information on its way to the prefrontal cortex and lends time and spatial context to memories of events. How well it functions determines the difference between normal and dysfunctional responses to stress and trauma and normal versus traumatic memory. An example will help to explain and may further clarify the James–Cannon controversy.

In his book *The Emotional Brain*, LeDoux (1996) described the survival response involved when, while taking a walk, you encounter an object that looks like a snake. Naturally, the amygdala signals a sub-cortical alarm message— "It's a snake!"—which sets in motion a series of reactions that culminates in your foot halting in midair. The amygdala's non-verbal message travels at lightning speed. Meanwhile, a second communication pathway occurs that takes longer, eventually getting the message around to the cortex, where rational and verbal thought takes place. When the alarm reaches the cortex along with the visual image of the object, it is then possible to evaluate the correctness of the amygdala's perception and put this evaluation into words. If the alarm was accurate and it is a snake, you will freeze until the danger has passed, that is, the snake slithers away. If, however, there is a discrepancy—what was thought to be a snake is discerned by the cortex to be a bent piece of wood—the cortex then sends a new message (often verbal) to the amygdala ("Hey, it's only a stick") to stop the alarm immediately.

The hippocampus, along with the thalamus, assists the transfer of the initial information—the image of stick or snake—to the cortex, where it is then possible to make sense of the situation. This is the normal way information is communicated, *as long as the hippocampus is able to function.*

How Stress Can Compromise Rational Thought

The hippocampus, however, is highly vulnerable to stress hormones, particularly epinephrine and norepinephrine, released by the amygdala's alarm. When those hormones reach a high level, they suppress the activity of the hippocampus; it loses its ability to function. Information that could make it possible to discern the difference between a snake and a stick never reaches the prefrontal cortex, and a rational evaluation of the situation is not possible.

The hippocampus is also a key structure in facilitating resolution and integration of highly stressful and traumatic incidents and traumatic memory. It inscribes a time context on events, giving each of them a beginning, middle, and—most important with regard to traumatic memory—an end. When stress hormone levels are reduced through control of hyperarousal, the hippocampus can come back to life, making it possible for the cortex to recognize when a traumatic event is over, perhaps even long past. Then it can instruct the amygdala to stop sounding an alarm. For the hippocampus to continue to function, SNS arousal levels must be kept low.

This means that for the psychotherapist to be able to think clearly, his hippocampus must be able to function. The therapist, then, must be able to "put on the brakes" to keep his SNS arousal low enough to ensure continued clear thinking.

MAKING SENSE AND THINKING CLEARLY

As explained above, the ability to speak and think clearly is compromised during trauma and in PTSD. Most relevant to the psychotherapist, those abilities also appear to be compromised by high levels of stress and vicarious trauma. It is advisable to make sure that you are always able to think clearly when working with clients (and probably in most other aspects of your life too). This means paying attention to your own levels of arousal and making sure it stays low enough that your hippocampus does not shut down. It is the function of the hippocampus, for example, to help you to distinguish whether an internal experience stems from something occurring now or something that occurred in the past. In this and other ways, the hippocampus assists your clear thinking.

It is important to remember that the function of the hippocampus is compromised by stress hormones; the more hormones are released, the higher the SNS hyperarousal and the greater the suppression of the hippocampus (Nadel & Jacobs, 1996). When the hippocampus is suppressed, you can no longer think clearly, as space and time become confused. Using mindfulness and putting on the brakes before the arousal becomes too high will help prevent this occurrence.

Another brain center important to a therapist's clear thinking is Broca's area, located in the left inferior frontal cortex. It helps us put experiences into words. This is another area affected by a rise in stress hormones due to hyperarousal. Suppression of Broca's area is the cause of what van der Kolk (1996) called the "speechless terror" of trauma—when, during trauma, an individual loses the ability to speak and make sense. This handicap can return during stressful circumstances when there are similar rises in arousal and hormone release. Needless to say, when a therapist becomes so distressed or vicariously traumatized that he is unable to think clearly, speak, or make verbal sense, his ability to help his clients becomes highly compromised and his own well-being is at risk.

SOMATIC MARKERS AND CLEAR THINKING

Usually people think that emotion interferes with rational thought, that it clouds their thinking. However, neurologist Antonio Damasio (1994) found that this is not the case. Actually, he proposed the opposite to be true: *Emotion is necessary to rational thought.*

Damasio describes an emotion as a conglomerate of sensations that are experienced in differing degrees, positive and negative. They make up the *somatic markers*, which help guide decision making. That is, body sensations that underlie emotions are the basis for weighing consequences, deciding direction, and identifying preferences.

The function of somatic markers is most recognizable in the kinds of choices people make every day based on gut feelings.

Damasio has worked with and studied individuals with damage to regions of the brain having to do with feeling emotion. He discovered that those whose brain damage eliminated or greatly diminished access to their feelings were no longer able to make good decisions. He concluded that feeling emotions is necessary to rational thought and decision making. Further, he found that it is body sensations (emotions) that cue awareness of feelings. Therefore, *to be able to make a rational decision, one must be able to feel the consequences of that decision in one's body.* According to Damasio, just projecting a cognitive judgment is not enough; it is the *feel* of it that counts.

Regulating your arousal to maintain clear thinking necessitates mindfulness and some experimentation. The following case will illustrate.

Toby has been a licensed clinical social worker in private practice for 6 years. This consultation was one in a series of regular biweekly consultation sessions.

Consultant: Start by telling me what you'd like to get from this consultation.

I often start a consultation this way. It helps me to attune my ears and my thinking to what the therapist wants or needs. When I forget this structure, often therapists will just begin to talk and it can be a long time before I gain perspective on why they are presenting this or that client. For those who like to talk without interference, it also saves me having to interrupt later.

Toby: I came today expecting to ask for strategies to help me work with a client who has been arrested twice for shoplifting. But actually, what I need is ways to manage the helplessness I feel with this client.

Consultant: Is it usual for you to feel helplessness with clients?

I wanted to know if this was a usual pattern for him, or something exceptional.

Toby: No, it's not normal for me to feel this way.
Consultant: What is "this way"?
Toby: I don't know that I can help her. In the sessions I lose my train of thought and have trouble staying focused. I feel ready to give up on her.
Consultant: In general, of course, we call that countertransference, whether it is usual or not. I think it is important to give your process the priority. So, actually, at this point, I don't need to know much about the client.

Sometimes when the focus is on countertransference, I find that too much information about the client can be a hindrance. At least, if I pursued details about the client's history at this point, we could lose precious time and get sidetracked from Toby's feelings of helplessness.

Toby: But I would like help to manage the client's lack of impulse control. Of course, she feels helpless too.
Consultant: I don't know if we will have time for all of that today. I'd suggest that we stick with your original request, your feelings of helplessness. Otherwise, if any therapeutic strategies we came up with for your client didn't work, you could find an increase in your feelings of helplessness.

Ultimately, it had to be Toby's choice, but I wanted to explain my thinking to him.

Toby: Yes, that makes sense.
Consultant: There are a couple of ways to go with this. Your helplessness with this client could have roots in your own history. However, since this is not a usual reaction for you, I would suspect that the origin lies elsewhere. At this point, I'd rather examine what is happening in your body as you work

with this client to assess if the helplessness stems from something in your interaction.

Toby: OK, I'll agree to that.

Consultant: Then let's begin with where you are right now. First, get a sense of your current somatic state. What are you aware of in your body and your feelings? I want to establish a baseline to compare with as we explore your countertransference—the feeling of helplessness—you brought up. Paying attention to your body will help to identify what could be *somatic countertransference.*

> *That is, countertransference on a body level: Body sensations or feelings that are provoked within the therapeutic encounter. Somatic countertransference may or may not have connection to something in the therapist's current or earlier life.*

Toby: I'm a little nervous here [*puts hand on chest*]. Also, I'm excited to get help with this.

> *Because he was nervous in his chest, I wanted to check for other signs of sympathetic arousal. I could see that his breathing was fairly relaxed.*

Consultant: How about temperature? What do you notice in your hands and feet?

Toby: They feel normal.

> *So his arousal was pretty low, maybe the nervousness is more from anticipation.*

Consultant: OK, now shift your awareness. Can you imagine that you're together with that client?

Toby: You want me to imagine being with the client now?

Consultant: Yes, if that's OK. You can do it with eyes open or closed. That's up to you. You might visualize the client if you are good at that kind of imagery. But it's OK if you don't see the client; the idea is to just have a sense of being with her. Can you do that?

Toby: [*closes eyes*] Yes. It's good you said that. I'm not good at visual imagery and was afraid I couldn't do it. But I can definitely get the feel of being with her.

Consultant: Great. Take a minute or so and then tell me what happens in your body as you imagine this client.

Toby: The nervousness increases in my chest, and my hands and feet have gone cold.

> *That meant his sympathetic nervous system was becoming more aroused. Remember, if the arousal becomes too high, hippocampal functioning can be lost. That might be what was happening with Toby, why he was losing his focus.*

Consultant: Continue to imagine being with your client and notice what's going on in your head. What kind of things are you saying to yourself?

Toby: Actually, my mind is sort of blank. It is not always easy for me to think with this client. I get drawn into what he's saying and then I can't think.

Consultant: Has anything changed in your body?

Toby: Well, actually, I can't feel it as much.

Consultant: What is the temperature of your hands and feet?

Toby: I think they are still cold, but I can't feel them as distinctly now.

> *If Toby became hyperaroused just by imagining being with this client, he likely also would become hyperaroused when actually with the client.*

Consultant: Sounds like you lost contact with yourself.

Toby: Maybe [*yawns*].

Consultant: Did you catch that you just yawned?

Toby: Now that you mention it, but I wasn't paying attention.

Consultant: So, stop imagining your client and talk with me. [*Toby shifts posture and his eyes clear.*] Is that typical when you are with this client, that you don't pay attention to yourself?

Toby: Yes, I think so. I get sort of numb.

Consultant: Do you think that could have a relationship to your feeling of helplessness with her?

Toby: Well, once I'm no longer thinking clearly, the helplessness just builds. And after the session I sometimes feel badly that I've not been able to help her more.

Consultant: If you could continue to think clearly, do you think you would feel as helpless?

Toby: I doubt it. I believe I have some tools to help her. I mainly lose track of what to do.

Consultant: Based on what happens in your body when you merely imagine being with her—the nervousness in your chest, your cold hands and feet, loss of contact with yourself—I suspect you are going into a high sympathetic arousal and losing the benefit of your hippocampus. If I am correct, then that is why you stop thinking clearly.

Toby: That's a little scary. Can I change that?

Consultant: Yes, of course. The key is to keep your arousal lowered when you are with her. Then your hippocampus will continue to function and it will be possible for you to think clearly. Let's try some things and see what might work. Based on what you said before, helping you to stay in touch with yourself will probably be important.

Sharing the theory should help Toby two ways: first to conceptualize what was happening within himself, and second to help his clients, who might also lose clarity due to hyperarousal. Now that he understood what was going on, it was time to see if he could intervene and get back his ability to think clearly with his client.

Toby: That sounds good. What should I do?

Consultant: Again, imagine being with your client and see what happens in your body.

Toby: Whew! The anxiety comes back very strongly and my feet and hands go cold again.

The arousal was triggered very quickly. That made me wonder what he might be doing to make himself more vulnerable. Taking a good look at his posture, I thought I might have a clue.

Consultant: I notice that you are sitting with one of your legs tucked under you. I wonder what would happen if you put both feet on the floor. Try that and see if anything changes for better or worse.

I must always be open to the possibility that an intervention will hurt rather than help. Every body is different, so you never really can know until you try. Asking in this way reduced the chance that Toby would feel led to a particular answer. I really wanted to know what would happen to him. If the result was good, we could build on it. If the result was bad, it could point us toward something else.

Toby: Well, first thing I notice, I can breathe easier. I hadn't realized I wasn't breathing much, but now I can. Should I still be imagining being with the client?

Consultant: Yes. That way we can pretest some things that might work. You won't know, though, until you actually try them with the client. Experimenting in this way can help you choose some things to do that will likely help. I'm glad that getting both feet on the floor was useful. Think of it as getting your feet under you—a more stable base. We can try taking that a step further. With your feet now under you, put some pressure on them so you tense up in your thighs. [*Toby complies.*] How's that?

Toby: Dunno. I feel a little spacey.

*When the result is increased arousal, spaciness, and so on,
then it is important to stop and go back to the intervention
that was useful.*

Consultant: Then stop doing that, and just feel your feet
on the floor.
Toby: OK, that's better. What happened?
Consultant: The only way to find out what helps you is to
experiment. When you get an adverse response like spacing
out or getting more anxious, you should stop doing it and
cross it off your list. Then go back to something that gave
a helpful response to get settled again. Then you can try
another.
Toby: I'm ready.
Consultant: What do you do with your hands when you see
this client?
Toby: Nothing in particular.

*I was wondering if doing something with his hands might
help secure his attention. Also, having objects in his hands,
like a notepad and pen, might also provide some physical
separation between him and his client.*

Consultant: Do you ever take notes?
Toby: I usually write up sessions after the client has gone.
Some of my clients don't like it when I take notes during the
session. Do you think I should?
Consultant: Remember, the idea is to find what works for
you. Taking notes might be something to test out. You can
assess for yourself if it is useful.
Toby: When I imagine doing that now, the notepad feels
like it is a sort of barrier between us. And my hands and feet
have warmed up a lot.
Consultant: That's a good response. The warmth in your
hands and feet means your sympathetic arousal is lowering
and your parasympathetic is rising. That's good news for your
hippocampus. I think that will be plenty for you to try out

with your client until our next consult: feet on the floor and taking notes. One last thing: Before you see her, check in with what is going on in your body so you have a baseline to compare with. Then during the session, do the same a couple of times. How will you remember?

Toby: I think I'm just going to start out with my notepad and feet on the floor. I'll write a note to myself at the top of the page.

Consultant: Next time I see you, I'll be curious about how it went.

> *Over the next few consultation sessions, Toby built on what was begun here. He continued to keep his feet on the floor and take notes, and he added a couple of muscle-toning exercises to thicken his skin. The combination of interventions worked to bring down his arousal with this difficult client. Once he was able to maintain clear thinking, his feelings of helplessness disappeared.*

SKILL BUILDING

Know Thyself

It will come as no surprise that it is a good idea for a psychotherapist to be familiar with her own life history. The better you know yourself, the greater the chance you will be able to maintain clear thinking when you are provoked by a client or a client's material. All therapists come face-to-face with their own personal issues at times during work with clients. Sometimes a therapist's own experience can be used to enhance the client's therapy. At other times it can interfere. The only way to ensure your ability to tell the difference is to know yourself—present and past—as well as possible. Accomplishing that may involve private soul-searching or it may mean having hours of your own therapy. Most psychotherapy educational programs now require a certain amount of personal therapy as part of the curriculum.

Being intimately familiar with your past will make it more likely that you will maintain clear thinking and easily distinguish your feelings and issues from your client's. Of course, having the opportunity to resolve problems that linger from your past can also be a bonus for your daily life. At the least, awareness of issues and problems not yet resolved will help to keep your thinking clear when your feelings become provoked in sensitive areas.

EXERCISE: TAKING A SELF-HISTORY

Certainly, many readers will already have had many hours of psychotherapy or in other ways have gotten to know themselves well. This section is written for those who have not yet delved into their past or would like guidance in deepening their self-knowledge.

One way to become familiar with your past is to write up your own history, asking yourself questions as you would a client to access your own past. It can be useful to write it down, but it is not necessary. The point is to know yourself at least as well as you know your clients, preferably better. Below are some suggested areas to include; this is not a complete survey. Feel free to bypass any questions, or add others.

1. Take note of your current living situation and marital status. Are you satisfied or not?
2. List any children and their ages. Comment on relationships between the family members as well as the family as a whole. Note the physical and mental health of each family member. Do you have any animals? If so, what role do they play in your life and in the family structure?
3. How is your own physical and mental health? Review your health history. Have you been hospitalized? Had surgery? Major injuries? Are there any serious concerns in either area that add to your daily stress?
4. List close friends and extended family members.

How are these relationships individually? On the whole, do you feel adequately supported in your life? Are you burdened by responsibilities of family and friends? What gives you pleasure with the people in your life? What gives you pain?

5. Describe your job and your workplace. Which aspects do you most and least enjoy? Are there coworkers or responsibilities that give you significant stress? If you are in private practice, do you have adequate collegial support? If you work in an agency, do you feel supported there? Are you satisfied with your chosen career? Do you wish for a different type of work or workplace? Do you look forward to retirement or not?

6. Consider your financial situation. Do you have adequate income or is this an area of stress for you?

7. Detail your family-of-origin constellation. Go back at least two generations, including grandparents. If it is complicated, draw a chart or genogram to be able to see the relationships. Indicate who is alive and who is not. For deceased family members, include how old they were at the time of death and what they died of.

8. List any life events with significant emotional charge: happy, sad, exciting, frightening, enraging, disgusting.

9. List any life-threatening events not covered by (8).

10. List any events of physical or sexual violence not covered by (8).

11. Include a review of your sexual history: how you heard about sex, how you managed puberty, first sexual experience, and so on, and your current sexuality.

12. Know your drug (legal and illegal) and alcohol history, and your current usage. Also pay attention to how much caffeine and sugar you consume.

13. Write down all medication you are currently taking, psychotropic and medical; include homeopathic remedies, vitamins, and other supplements.

14. If you have or have had bouts of depression or bipolar episodes, look for patterns. Include planning, attempts, or gestures of suicide.
15. Pay attention to any spiritual beliefs, whether or not they are part of an organized system. Also, note your relationship to nature.

Once you have all of your personal information put together, in your mind or on paper, consider if there are any issues or areas that enhance your professional competence and any that might compromise it. Also make note of areas that parallel issues any of your clients have, whether or not they are currently working on them. Look for common themes that might give you difficulties and also those that could give you advantages.

Next consider your religious, political, and moral values. Are any of your values in conflict with those of your clients? If so, how are you handling that, or how will you handle it when it comes up?

Finally, when you discover you are having difficulty with a client, you can refer back to what you know about yourself to see if any parallels or triggers are causing you difficulty (as Ruth does in Chapter 5). When they are, sometimes just that knowledge will be enough to separate your issues from your client's. If that is ·the case, your thinking will clear quickly and work with that client will be less difficult. However, if awareness is not enough, talking with your supervisor or a psychotherapist may be indicated.

Strengthening the Observer

Psychoanalysis calls it the *observing ego;* transactional analysis calls it the *adult;* van der Kolk (van der Kolk et al., 1996) called it the *observing self.* Buddhists call it the *witness,* and other disciplines have names unknown to this author. Here it will simply be called the *observer.* No matter what name you give it, though, this is an integral part of the self and crucial to clear thinking. The observer is able to view and simultaneously evaluate both external and internal reality. Adequate functioning of the observer is vital to emotional health—for psychotherapists, their clients, and everyone else. Without a strong observer, it can be all too easy for therapists to confuse the stresses, feelings, and states of clients with their own.

DUAL AWARENESS

Having dual awareness means being able to simultaneously attend to and reconcile both external (from exteroceptors) and internal (from interoceptors) sensory information (you can review these systems in Chapter 2). It is an important ability to maintain under stress—for anyone, but especially for a psychotherapist. Without dual awareness, clear thinking is not possible. It is a skill made possible by the effective functioning of the hippocampus and prefrontal cortex, and is facilitated by keeping SNS arousal low enough. When these brain regions can do their jobs, you will be better able to do yours.

Normally, dual awareness functions automatically in the background, unconsciously. We are usually not aware of it. Basically, dual awareness reconciles all of the information we are taking in through our sensory nervous system: both the exteroceptors (what I see, hear, etc.) and the interoceptors (balance, position, internal sensations, etc.). The exteroceptors register information from the external environment and the interoceptors gather information from our internal systems. When all goes well, your internal state is in sync with your awareness of your surroundings. A few examples follow:

- You are walking in your favorite place in nature on a beautiful day. Your exteroceptors are picking up on the light, warmth, bird sounds, brush crunching under your feet; the whole scene is peaceful. At the same time, your interoceptors register the relaxed state of your gut, your deep breaths, your steady balance and pace. All is well on the inside and the outside.

- Sitting in a room with friends, you notice that your heart rate has increased and your chest has become tight (interoceptor). You wonder why. You turn your awareness to your external environment and notice the smell (exteroceptor) of cigarette smoke and locate by sight (exteroceptor) the source as a cigarette held by someone sitting near you. You remember that you are allergic to cigarette smoke and move to the other side of the room. The exteroceptive perception (someone smoking) reconciles with your internal sense of tight chest and elevated heart rate (both triggered by second-hand smoke).

- Later with the same friends, your chest becomes tight and your heart rate increases once again. What is it this time? You turn your awareness outward but do not smell anything aversive or see anyone smoking. What else could it be? You pay closer attention to the conversation and hear (exteroceptor) that the current topic is workplace deadlines. You remember that your boss has been after you to turn in a report and you realize you are anxious since you have not yet done it.

In all of these examples, the exteroceptive information reconciles with the interoceptive, as is usual. But this is not always the case. When maintaining simultaneous attention to internal and external cues is difficult, reconciliation will be hampered and your risk for vicarious trauma or burnout could be increased.

PTSD is the poster child for the failure of dual awareness. When the capacity for simultaneous attention to the internal and external is lost, dual awareness is no longer possible. In that case, a bias develops in favor of either the external environment or the internal environment. Rothschild (2000, 2003) has described failures of dual awareness in individuals with PTSD. In those cases, the bias is toward the internal cues of fear. Restriction in the lives of those with PTSD is partially the result of a reliance on internal (interoceptive) cues to define external reality. These individuals lose touch with the value of their exteroceptors. In extreme cases, victims of PTSD conclude that their surroundings are dangerous because they feel scared all the time. They lose the ability to use exteroceptors to accurately evaluate the external environment by what they see, hear, and so on. Because of that, their fear regenerates and regenerates. They are unable to use exteroceptors to recognize when they are actually safe. Certainly, therapists can fall into that same pattern, especially those who already have PTSD or vicarious trauma.

Failure of dual awareness in psychotherapists is best illustrated by situations where a therapist jumps to conclusions: "I'm feeling scared, so my client must be doing something dangerous (or threatening)"; or "I'm feeling irritated, so my client must be doing something provocative (or wrong)." In such cases the issue is not the client's behavior, but the therapist's misinterpretation of internal sensation. (Remember the example of how the amygdala reacted to a stick as if it was a snake.) Often the consequence is inappropriate confrontation of the client, resulting in confusion and frustration for both client and therapist. While such loops in logic are not terribly common, they occur often enough. Many readers will have taken on new clients who had recently discharged a therapist after being unable to resolve such a situation. Some may have experienced this themselves in their own therapy. Most of us have gotten at least a few new clients in this way.

There is an additional way that failure of dual awareness can manifest that practitioners should be alert for. The opposite can occur. That is, psychotherapists can become overly reliant on the external environment to dictate what they should be doing. Psychotherapists, like most helping professionals, are caretakers by nature. Many of us have cared for our families beginning in early childhood, or are the primary caretaker in our current family. We are, for the most part, used to putting others first. This tendency is definitely a resource as it helps us to have interest, energy, and focus for dealing with difficult client material. It gives us endurance and an ability to ignore or put aside our interoceptive sensations of tiredness or stress when we believe another's needs must come first. But it can also be a deficit if we allow that tendency to override our own needs for rest, debriefing, emotional expression, diversion, and so on.

The story of Bonnita Wirth (see Chapter 3) is a good example of an exteroceptive bias. She lost contact with her body and the interoceptive signs that could have alerted her to the fact that she was not sleeping well. Luckily, she made a cognitive decision to change paths before she actually did succumb to burnout.

When a therapist is biased in favor of the external environment, there can be a serious loss of contact with the internal self and the gauges of self-regulation that are also centered there. If contact with the interoceptors has been weakened, for example, a therapist might not pay attention to signs of stress, tiredness, or overload. In fact, exteroceptive bias in therapists might be a major risk factor in burnout. In addition, when internal emotional states such as fear or anxiety do not come into awareness or are ignored, practitioners could put themselves in dangerous situations (e.g., accepting violent clients without adequate protection).

It is important to keep in mind that feelings are an aggregate of interoceptive sensations and states and that they are survival mechanisms. Fear alerts us to danger; anger tells us that we are being pushed too far, and so on. Acknowledging our feelings is crucial for keeping us safe and otherwise able to care for ourselves. Turning off one system in favor of another is risky.

Thus, for therapist self-care, dual awareness—being able to take into account information from all systems—will contribute to decreased professional risks for compassion fatigue, vicarious trauma, and burnout, not to mention increasing overall safety.

EXERCISE: DUAL AWARENESS IN THE SESSION

This technique is very useful for quickly putting on the brakes when high arousal is threatening hippocampal function (or has already). It can also be useful when you find it difficult to keep your concentration or your attention. As for most of the other skills described in this book, having a baseline gauge of body awareness before you start a session can be very helpful. When, during a session, you identify the pull of your interoceptors—rising arousal, anxiety, feeling uncomfortably drawn into what your client is working on, or floundering attention—fall back on dual awareness. Turning on your exteroceptors can help remind you where you actually are and what is currently happening. Such action can restore clear thinking quite rapidly. This is one instance where working in a noisy office can have advantages. You can use the (often) irritating distraction as an exteroceptive ally to connect you to the here and now.

For those who have a quiet office or want additional tools, it can be useful to designate one or more items in your office to be your in-session reminder. You can choose a picture, a knick-knack, your computer—anything. Looking at or holding a successful reminder will keep you in or bring you back to clear thinking when you lose touch with yourself, or if you become triggered into distress. It is called a reminder because, by turning on one or more exteroceptors, it reminds you of the here and now. Sometimes it is useful to choose a reminder that is active, a procedure like counting the panes in a window or lights in the ceiling. The idea is to have a kind of "power object" or activity that can help you to remain rooted in the now, in yourself, and in your office rather than slipping into your or your client's past or distress. While it can facilitate your client's therapy for you to have a sense of something being triggered in your past or a feeling for the issue your client is working with, becoming immersed in it can be detrimental for both you and your client. As the therapist, you always need to maintain awareness of where you are—dual awareness—so that you will be able to continue to think clearly. A common sense rule of thumb for therapist self-care: Make sure that one person in the therapy room is thinking clearly at all times. Because you cannot expect your client to be that person, you had best ensure that it is you.

The more you get accustomed to using your dual awareness reminder, the more useful it will be for you during stressful times with clients. A successful reminder will both calm you and clear your thinking. To practice, first think of something slightly distressing and notice how that distress feels in your body. Next, make contact with your reminder and see if sensations of distress weaken or disappear. If they do, you have chosen a reminder that works well for you. You will know if you need to choose a different reminder if there is no change or your distress increases.

If using a visual reminder is not effective for you, try a tactile one: your pencil, a stone in your pocket, the texture of your clothing, or your chair's upholstery, for example.

EXERCISE: CONTAINER CONSTRUCTION

Clients bring us upsetting material on a regular basis. One of the most common functions of the psychotherapist is to hold what the client cannot. Usually this happens in an abstract way when clients tell us their troubles or describe the painful or horrific things they have experienced. However, many therapists—both consciously and unconsciously—continue to carry around client material throughout their workday and on into their private lives. If thoughts of clients, their problems, or history intrude into your free time, you may be holding too much of your clients in your mind-body system. Some therapists believe that this is what they are supposed to do, not noticing whether or not their habit causes any ill effects. Though the effect of carrying around client material is sometimes benign, thinking or worrying about your clients between sessions may indicate a possible problem. If you discover that your sleep is being regularly disturbed by dreams of clients or you are having nightmares similar to your client's, you are certainly carrying around too much. A strategy for containing and then putting aside client material was inspired by one of my own clients.

Roger was sexually abused repeatedly as a young child by a neighbor. He felt very ashamed and never told anyone until he entered therapy as an adult. He had managed to wall off that part of himself and went on to have a fairly successful life. When his own son became a toddler, however, Roger began to have anxiety attacks and episodes in which feelings of shame—being dirty and repulsive—would overwhelm him.

One weekend, Roger helped his son with finger paints; together they made pictures. That day, his son was only interested in the brown colors, many shades of brown. Roger enjoyed painting with his son and went on to paint his own picture in browns. He really got into it, realizing he was putting all of his self-loathing into the painting. The next week he brought it to me, completely crunched up in a plastic bag. "Here," he said. "Keep this for me. I don't want these feelings anymore!" Together we decided I would keep the bag in the back of my file cabinet. He never asked for it back. Actually, I even forgot about it for several years until I came across it while cleaning out my files.

That experience gave me an idea that has proved useful for myself and for some of the therapists I supervise and teach: Put distressing client material in a *container* and leave it in the file cabinet (or somewhere else secure) between sessions, at the end of the day, over weekends, and during vacations. *Don't carry it with you.*

Many psychotherapists already use the idea of creating a

container with their clients, helping them to put aside and manage distressing memories or thoughts on a daily basis or between sessions. But we do not usually think of using the same strategy for our own benefit when clients leave their distressing feelings and memories with us—that is, when we find ourselves overly preoccupied by a client following or between sessions, or even after discharge. Creating a container can be useful for us, too.

The potential container can be a real physical container, like Roger's bag. It can be something sturdier: a box, a safe, or a file drawer. You might also create a container in your imagination, so long as the imagined container feels real enough to you and does the trick, effectively holding what you want it to. You will recognize an adequate container by using your body awareness to gauge your arousal, and by checking to see if your thinking remains clear.

I will use myself for one of the case examples, along with two of my trainees, to describe instances in which this skill has proved effective. However, please take note that the success of creating a container largely depends on your own creativity in creating it and belief in its adequacy, so resist any urge to just copy from these examples. Create your own container that is personally suited to you.

Usually my file cabinet does the trick. In it I have a folder for each client. It is also where I store my notepad overnight and on weekends. So any and all information about my clients is kept there. As is usually recommended, it has a lock for general security. That lock is also an added benefit when I use the file cabinet as my container. After a particularly demanding day, or when I have a client who is preoccupying my mind, I make a minor ceremony out of putting away my files and notes, and turning my key in the lock. Sometimes just the physical act of storing the mater-

ial and locking up is enough. When that is not adequate, I will add an action or some words. Once I brushed my hair and left the brush in the drawer; I felt as if I was clearing the cobwebs from my mind and leaving them locked up for the night. The next morning when I found the brush, some of the concerns about a particular client that had been unresolved fell into place. Another time a particularly clingy client gave me a small gift. Usually I will leave such a thing on display on a shelf. But this object kept dragging my attention back to that client. It was inconvenient. I decided to keep the object in the file cabinet and only brought it out when the client came for a session. It was a good compromise; the client was not offended and I was no longer bothered.

A psychologist who attended one of my training courses asked for help with ruminations about one of his clients. For at least a full day following sessions with the client in question, the psychologist would continue thinking about him during session breaks and in the evening. Sometimes thoughts of this client would keep the therapist awake the night after a session. We developed a twofold strategy that proved useful. First the therapist agreed to arrange to debrief with a colleague shortly after each of these sessions (so the colleague became a container). Second, the psychologist constructed an especially sturdy file folder for that client's papers. He broke down a packing box and used the flat sides, cutting and taping to make a 9" × 12" × 3" container with a flap. After talking with the colleague, he would take the client's file and any additional notes and put them in the cardboard file, wrap it with sturdy string, and place it in his office closet. He would leave it there until shortly before the next session when he would take it out and review his notes. After doing this religiously for a few weeks, one evening he was rushed and forgot to pack up thoroughly. The next day he realized that he was free of client ruminations even without using the cardboard con-

*tainer, and he laid it aside. He continued, however, to de-
brief with his colleague and utilize supervision until the
underlying countertransference issues were resolved.*

*One of the clinical social workers attending a training
program discussed a strategy she uses on a regular basis
following sessions with trauma clients. She often hears
horrendous incidents of rape, physical and sexual abuse,
and torture. For too many years she would suffer anxiety
and sometimes nightmares after hearing the details of such
incidents. On the advice of a colleague, she bought a beautiful box with a volume of about 2 square feet. She found
it at a yard sale and was told it was jewelry box (evidently
for someone with a lot of jewels), so it had a lock and key.
The social worker located the box in a corner of her office
and placed a small cactus on it. After sessions in which terrible stories were told, she would move the cactus and open
the box. She imagined all the horrible things she had heard
being sucked into the box, embellishing her fantasy with
visual and auditory effects. Sometimes she would make
motions to sweep those things into the box as well. When
she felt satisfied that the distressing material was fully
loaded, she would close the lid, lock the box with the key,
put the key in the bottom drawer of her locking file cabinet,
and replace the cactus on top of the box. She knew when
she had effectively packed all of the distress into the box
as it no longer dogged her throughout her day or night.*

Obviously an element of belief is necessary for the effective use of this kind of container strategy. For those who find
this kind of tool appealing, it can be very useful. However,
do not be daunted if this one is not for you.

EXERCISE: PHYSICAL EXERCISE

Those in professions involving high emotional and physical
stress, particularly police, firefighters, and the like, know that
physical exercise (working out, sports, etc.) helps them to re-

duce stress and maintain clear thinking. Psychotherapists can also benefit from a regular schedule of exercise or sports. Any way you can use your body to let off steam, increase muscle strength, promote endurance, and so on will help you to clear your head and better manage the stresses of your work. The key is to find something that is pleasant for you to do on a regular basis: walking, running, swimming, playing tennis, digging in the garden, working out, yoga, tai chi, anything that works for you. Sometimes it is difficult to get started with regular exercise, but once you get in the habit, it quickly becomes self-rewarding. If you can interest a colleague, friend, or your partner in joining you, then the benefit multiplies with the camaraderie.

Controlling Self-Talk

Considering how clients speak to themselves inside their heads, specifically what they say, is a common intervention in psychotherapy. This practice originated as a cognitive-behavioral strategy. Most of you will have used such an intervention with one or more clients. Usually we do this to help clients understand that how and what they think can affect how they feel (the other side of the James-Cannon debate). Of course, the same applies to the psychotherapist: How you regard your clients, what you hear from your clients, and how you judge your own competency will have a significant bearing on how your work affects you. Basically, this is common sense. If you think of yourself as competent in your work, you will have a better feeling about it than if you judge yourself as largely falling short. Likewise, when you use language that increases your identification with your client, it will be harder to find a comfortable separation.

REDUCING IDENTIFICATION

Sometimes the simplest intervention is the most powerful. When in doubt, it is almost always worth trying. However, the simplest solution might not be obvious unless you are using your common sense. When your internal dialog is phrased to increase identification with your clients, it can also simultaneously put you at risk. The only way to know if what you tell yourself is having a negative impact on you is to experiment, trying identification oriented dialog with some clients and separation oriented dialog with others.

> *Rich is a gay psychotherapist with a general practice of both straight and gay clients. Contrary to what one might assume, he actually finds his gay clients more emotionally demanding to work with. The days that include a majority of gay clients are usually more stressful and exhausting for Rich. He noticed the pattern himself and it bothered him a great deal. Having so much in common with his gay clients should, he thought, be an asset, not a handicap. He judged himself to be overly sensitive and worried that he was ill suited to work with a gay population.*
>
> *During a consultation session, we took a look at why Rich was having so much difficulty. He confided that his own sexual coming of age had been difficult; most of his family had difficulty accepting him after he came out. Though that was some years ago, he still had emotional scars that stung. Rich felt especially close to his gay clients but was beginning to worry that such closeness actually hampered his ability to help them. At the least, he knew it had a cost for his own well-being.*
>
> *Could a simple intervention help Rich? Based on how he talked about his clients and his own competence, I became suspicious that his internal dialogue could be compounding his problems. Rich confirmed that he mentally used phrases in silent response to his client's reports that increased his identification with them: "like what happened to me" "like I sometimes feel" and so on.*
>
> *It is often expedient to start with the simplest thing, and that is what I suggested to Rich. I proposed that he try a new internal mantra during sessions with one or two of his gay clients in the next week: "I have experienced things*

like this client has, but he is not me. His problems are his and not mine, and right now it is his turn to get help."

Admittedly, Rich was suspicious of my simple idea, but he agreed to try it. At the next consultation, he reported that he was somewhat less stressed. He thought that the mantra might be helping but wasn't sure. Seeing as he was feeling a bit better, though, he decided to keep using it. Rich himself suggested adding another mantra: "I may not be able to help [my client], but that doesn't mean I am incompetent," which also led us to a discussion about his feelings of responsibility for his clients' welfare, what was reasonable, and what was not.

Over the next few weeks, Rich became adept at finding different ways to think about his clients and his work with them during the sessions and in between. His stress eased to a large extent and his thinking cleared.

This minimal intervention worked well for Rich, but it will not for everyone. However, in my experience, it is useful often enough to belong on the list of possible interventions to experiment with.

SELF-CRITICISM

Chronic self-criticism can be as debilitating for a psychotherapist as for anyone. At the least, it hampers effectiveness and clear thinking. Sometimes simple tools will not be enough to stem the internal onslaught and other interventions will be necessary.

Mason had recently received an MA in counseling. He was hired by a local agency to provide psychotherapy to a general population. Mason's training had all been top-notch and he had received both good grades and good evaluations in graduate school. While his tendency toward self-depreciation had kept him working hard in school, it was now becoming debilitating as his internal critic escalated. No longer preoccupied with homework in

*the evenings and on weekends, Mason found he was
spending inordinate amounts of time reviewing client sessions and finding fault with himself. The internal dialogue
seemed unstoppable. Mason was becoming more and
more troubled. His insightful supervisor was used to
hearing Mason's tendency to self-criticism. Usually he
didn't think much about it, as it appeared Mason was doing a fairly good job with his clients. But when the supervisor noticed a change in Mason's demeanor, he asked
about it.*

*Frankly, the supervisor was shocked to discover just how
severe and active Mason's inner critic was. They discussed
the situation and agreed that adequate intervention was
beyond the scope of the supervisory relationship and that
Mason could probably benefit from some personal psychotherapy. Likely, it would not be a short-term course, as
the roots reached back to his childhood and family of origin. But Mason felt encouraged to be supported in taking
this step.*

STORIES OF TRAUMA

Sometimes client stories provoke arousal and upset even
when there is no shared history between therapist and client.
Especially when working with trauma, the stories clients tell
can be particularly disturbing.

*Aris is a psychologist in a center for tortured and trau-
matized refugees. Daily, she hears recountings of terrible
acts that were done to her clients. Highly committed to her
clientele, there are times when Aris feels guilty that her
life has been so easy in comparison. She has never experienced anything even remotely so awful. Sometimes she
fears that she can't relate enough to what has happened to
her clients to really be able to help them. At those times,
she often finds herself describing to herself in detail what
it would be like if some of those things happened to her. As
a result, Aris is prone to nightmares about captivity and
torture that are starting to encroach on her ability to func-*

tion in her daily life.

Her supervisor, who had been doing the same work twice as long as Aris, gently suggested that Aris stop attempting to identify with her clients. In the supervisor's experience, that kind of descriptive identification was much more hurtful than helpful. They discussed the pros and cons of sharing client experiences. Aris was helped to see that her less traumatic life history gave her a stability and positive life view that potentially could be useful to her clients. The supervisor also recommended that Aris remind herself often that those horrible experiences were her clients', not her own, to consciously make that separation.

That simple intervention stopped Aris's nightmares. But it took several more months of discussions with her supervisor to fully make peace with the differences in her and her clients' backgrounds.

EXERCISE: SELF-TALK

Identify one client with whom you feel stressed during or following sessions.

1. Write down at least three phrases that describe how you feel about yourself when you are working with this client.
2. During your next session with this client, pay attention to the thoughts that go through your mind, what you say to yourself about yourself, your client, your work. Write them down. It may help to keep a piece of paper separate from your client notes for this purpose. It is important to record the phrases so that you can later look at them concretely and objectively.
3. Take a look at both sets of phrases (1 and 2 above). One at a time, determine if a particular phrase has an enabling or disabling effect on you.
4. Read a phrase aloud or just say it in your mind and

feel the impact it has on your body and your feelings:
Do you become more or less calm? More tense or
less? Does your mood lighten or darken?

5. If you feel a pleasant effect, make a note of that and
move on to the next phrase.

6. When you find a phrase that has an uncomfortable effect, rewrite it. Change the phrase to something that
makes you feel neutral or better rather than worse. You
can use the example of Rich, above, who changed his
feeling of incompetence by recognizing that he would
not be able to help everyone.

7. Take one or two of your rewritten phrases into the
next session with your client. During the session, use
that phrase in your mind and see if and how it affects
you. Do you respond differently than you did to the
original phrase? Does the new phrase help or hinder
your professional competence? Does it help or hinder your clear thinking?

8. If you like the result, continue to use the new phrase.
If you do not like the result, do not use it.

9. Try this with at least two phrases for each of three
clients before you decide whether this type of skill
is useful for you or not.

EXERCISE: INTERNAL SUPERVISION

- List the three most disabling things you have ever
  heard from a supervisor. Do you say any of these to
  yourself? If so, why?
- List the three most enabling things you have heard
  from a supervisor. Do you say any of these to yourself? If not, why not?
- Make a list of helpful "internal supervisor" feedback
  you can regularly give to yourself.

Nurturing Your Work Space

Look around your work space. What do you need to change, add, or remove to make it a more nurturing space for you? Most of us spend approximately one third of our lives in our work space. It should be comfortable and nourishing. Consider: How are things arranged? What are you usually looking at? How does the furniture you usually sit on feel to your body? What about clutter? Are there areas that need cleaning up? Or, the opposite, is your space too sterile? Do you need to add clutter or cozy touches? Do you like greenery or flowers? If so, how about adding some to your space? Or tropical fish? Are your window coverings adequate—enough light and enough privacy?

A couple of years ago, frustrated in a new office, I realized I needed an electric kettle so I did not need to go down the hall to make tea. Just having that within my reach helped me to feel much more cozy and cared for in my office. It was a simple, inexpensive change that made a big difference.

For those of you who work in different spaces throughout a day or week, what can you take with you that will add to your feeling of being cared for and nurtured? For instance, some clinicians carry favorite pictures, stones, or other talismans with them to enhance their feeling of continuity from place to place. Whatever it is, take the time and budget the money necessary to feel cared about in the place where you work. The more comfortable you feel in your work space, the clearer your thinking will be.

Structured Self-Care

Structure and planning ahead can be allies when it comes to taking adequate care of yourself. Remember, adequate self-care ensures greater calm and clear thinking—a bonus for both you and your clients. For the following exercise, use a new sheet of paper so you will be able to post your responses in a place where you will see the paper. This will help you remember to do the things you planned. At the end of each task is a list of hints to inspire your own list. These are only meant for inspiration and by no means include all of the possible things that you might do for yourself. You are welcome to send me an e-mail with your own ideas and strategies to pass on to others.

These plans can relate to your work with clients, your work with supervisees, or your interactions with colleagues. The term *session* is meant to refer to any of these situations. If it is relevant for you, make separate lists for the first two categories as they apply to different situations.

Below are the categories, with inspiration from others who have done this exercise. The suggestions are only to give you an idea of what kinds of things might be important.

1. List three or more things that you will pay attention to during each session:

   Position

   Facial expression

   Breathing pattern

   Body sensations

   Arousal level

   Areas that need more muscle tone

   Self-talk

2. Assess for each new client or those with whom you have difficulty: What do I need when I am with this client?

   A thicker skin

   Increased muscle tone

   To feel my edges

   To feel my feet

Remind myself that she is not me

Remind myself that his story is not my story

3. List three or more things that you will do between each session:

Write some notes

Open a window

Get a (warm) drink

Go to the restroom

Wash hands

Stretch

Tone up muscles

Do a cleansing ritual

Listen or dance to music

Eat a snack

4. List three or more things that you will do at the end of each day or each evening:

Put client and/or colleague material in a secure container

Take a shower

Say evening prayers

Yell out the car window

Call or talk to a friend

Exercise

Read the paper

Watch some television

Read a good book

Change clothes

5. List three or more things that you will do (at least) one time each week:

Get exercise

Have sex

See a movie

Visit with friends or family

Do volunteer work not related to my employment

Get out in nature

Do something artistic

Have the weekend free to do fun or nurturing things

6. List three or more things that you will do (at least) biweekly or monthly:

See your own therapist

Talk with a supervisor or consultant

Take a minivacation

Have or attend a party

7. Now, decide two things:

Who you will discuss these plans with (partner, friend, colleague, therapist, supervisor)

Where you will post your list (or parts of it) so that you will see it and be reminded to follow your plan

FUTURE TEMPLATE

Imagine yourself on your job in the future. One at a time, imagine problems that might arise and make plans for how you would tackle each. Write down your strategies and make note of where you might need more information or more practice.

NEW CLIENT ASSESSMENT

With each new client, as part of your normal assessment, ask yourself, "What do I need to look after myself with this client? What are the issues that this client might trigger for me? Which characteristics or styles does this client have that I need to be prepared for?" Consider all of the things you have learned from this book (self-talk, muscle tone, mirroring, etc.) as well as prior tools.

Cleansing Rituals

I have heard reports from many practitioners that following sessions with particular clients, it seems as if the clients are still sticking to their skin. For that and similar feelings, when it seems a client is still hanging around, cleansing rituals can be helpful.

Washing hands is the most obvious and most common cleansing ritual (used consciously and unconsciously). Many therapists routinely visit the restroom between sessions, sometimes only to wash their hands. Others prefer to cleanse the room's atmosphere by opening a window or door and airing it out. When that is not possible or preferable, spraying scents or burning a candle, incense, or dried herbs (sage is often used for this purpose) may be an option—of course for any of these you need to be respectful of fire safety, office rules, and coworker and client allergies.

For some, imagined cleansing—of the room or their person—is useful. I have been told about several:

- A gentle wind that cleans the air and lingering distress from the room.
- A shower of water or energy that rinses off all traces of the client and session from the skin.
- Going for a walk or run somewhere in nature.
- Swimming in cool water.

This list is by no means complete. I have included it only as inspiration for you to find your own. As with many sorts of rituals, the success of a cleansing ritual relies on belief. You have to choose or create one that makes sense to you and suits the needs of your body and mind. Try several before you settle on one or two.

HOME FREE: END-OF-THE-DAY RITUALS FOR LEAVING WORK AT WORK

Do you practice any kind of ritual at the end of the day to mark the end of work and the beginning of leisure? It can be a good idea to be aware of what you might already be doing or to create a new ritual for yourself. The goal is for you to really leave your work and clients at your workplace, so that your free time is really free. That includes evenings, weekends, and vacations. Many practitioners need something concrete to do to make the transition from work to free time. Some of the things they do include taking a shower, having a glass of wine, changing shoes, changing clothes, listening to music on the trip home, saying evening prayers on the trip home, sealing client files in a drawer or file cabinet, talking to a friend, partner, or colleague about their day, and so on. Do some experimenting to find what works for you.

Note that this section, as well as this entire book, has focused on the impact of practicing psychotherapy on the psychotherapist. Both theory and skill-building interventions are aimed at maximizing the therapist's self-care in relationship to his work. Of course, other aspects of a therapist's life are also relevant to overall well-being and self-care. Family issues, financial problems, illness (personal or a loved one's), just to name a few, can all deeply affect any individual, including a psychotherapist. Addressing aspects of the professional's personal life, however, is beyond the scope of this book.

Chapter 5

Concluding Reflections

This chapter will wrap-up and tie together the ideas laid out in the forgoing pages. The first section will conclude the discussion on projective identification that was begun in Chapter 1. Next, an in-depth case study will demonstrate one way in which the theories and skills covered in this text have been creatively applied. Lastly, a few final words will end the text portion of this book.

REVISITING PROJECTIVE IDENTIFICATION

By now readers have likely realized that I am leery of the theory of projective identification as a way to understand the impact of a client's emotions on the psychotherapist. In this, I am not alone. Some psychoanalysts even eschew the concept, cautioning that it provides fertile ground for client blame and avoidance of therapist responsibility (Grotstein, 1981; Whipple, 1986). Looking to cognitive, emotional, and somatic empathy for the source of the phenomenon provides a more logical and more liberating explanation. Paying attention to somatic empathy and all that it encompasses makes it possible to put the psychotherapist in charge of her own feelings, sensations, and behaviors—even when she is with difficult clients.

Since its inception, many psychotherapists, including Grotstein (1981) and Schore (2002) have found the concept of projective identification to be confusing, at best an enigma. At the same time, others have embraced it as a foundational theory of their practice. In *Narcissism and Intimacy*, Marion Solomon voiced a commonly held interpretation of Klein's theory: "The process involves psychologically transferring a piece of oneself *into* another and then *inducing the other to behave* in accordance with the projection" (1989, p. 88, italics mine). Others, Schore (2003), Stark (1999), and Grinberg (1979) among them, have similar beliefs about the power of one person over another, including the patient's power over the therapist. Following that idea, a therapist might believe that her own critical outburst—or other inappropriate behavior—can be induced by her client's unconscious need. Unfortunately, many of today's psychoanalysts and psychotherapists believe that clients can, and do, control therapists' feelings and actions. That the phenomenon of projective identification occurs is not up for dispute. What is disputable, however, is the mechanism. From the bulk of literature on the topic, it seems that projective identification is perceived as an active process on the part of the client and a passive one on the part of the analyst. Both notions can be challenged.

When a therapist falls back on projective identification to understand her own discomfort with a client, she may endanger both of them. The client may be unfairly blamed, and the therapist may end up feeling a helpless victim. Adhering to such a belief can leave a psychotherapist all the more vulnerable to the consequences of compassion fatigue, vicarious trauma, and burnout.

Rooted in the understanding of empathy, including facial and postural mirroring (for a review, see Chapter 2), empathic imagery (Chapter 3), and identifying self-talk (Chapter 4) what has been believed to be projection for more than 50 years may now be seen as the therapist's empathetic response within herself. Identifying the active mechanism of projective identification as something inside the therapist puts her firmly in the driver's seat to control how much, how often, how intensely, she will resonate with her client's feelings. This makes it possible to prevent, or at least relieve, ill effects from resonance.

Contrary to many of his colleagues, Stolorow and associates (2002) found the theory of projective identification outmoded and outdated. He described projective identification as "one of the last, seemingly unassailable strongholds of Cartesianism in relational psychoanalysis" (p. 88). He went on to point out that therapists who subscribe to the theory of projective identification are mistakenly "inferring causation from correlation" (p. 91). He believed that two people (spouses, therapist and client, etc.) can have the same feeling (correlation) without one inducing it in the other (causation). That is, the fact of shared feelings does not prove that one *caused* the feelings in the other. As discussed in the section Somatic Empathy in Chapter 2, people are affected by the emotions of others all the time, usually inadvertently. *Being affected by another's emotion is not the same as having an emotion induced or put into you.*

If a psychotherapist is to mediate his own compassion fatigue, vicarious trauma, or burnout, he needs to recognize that he is not helpless to resist induction of the emotional states of his clients. Such a belief undermines the therapist's power to choose. The therapist who believes he is his client's pawn puts his own well-being at great risk. He is also at risk of harming the very people he endeavors to help, if only by blaming them for his discomfort.

Of course, emotions can be communicated, sent and received. That is the main theme throughout this book. But they cannot be induced. Certainly, the therapist's ability to resonate with or experience her client's feelings can be a valuable tool. However, if she perceives herself as an involuntary recipient with no control over reception, then the therapeutic relationship and her own emotional health will suffer.

Some clues to how to control unconscious mirroring— when it is believed to be projective identification—are provided by Martha Stark (1999) in *Modes of Therapeutic Action*. Stark believed her analytic patients "get me to" (p. 266) do all sorts of things that she would not otherwise do: experience feelings, act out behaviors, and so on. A few pages later, though, she acknowledged that the analyst can get herself out of the projection by "either a subtle (and often unconscious) shift or a more dramatic (and sometimes more conscious) *shift in her position*" (p. 276, italics mine) or by taking a "step back" (p. 283) to recover impartiality. While Stark was referring to cognitive processes for regaining objectivity (shifting position and stepping back) such as dual awareness, it is even more effective to take her advice literally: When you find yourself being infected by a client's emotions, step away (step back) or shift position to break the body-to-body resonance. For good measure, stepping back or shifting position *both* physically *and* mentally will give the therapist a powerful way to distance herself from the client's affective space (for a review of additional strategies, see Unmirroring in Chapter 2).

TO EACH HER OWN CHAIR

In her exceptional book, *In the Other Chair*, Yvonne Tauber (1998) illuminated the difficulties involved when Holocaust survivors and their children ("Second Generation") are psychotherapists for those in the same populations. While those are specialized pairings, many of the same hazards apply to all sorts of therapeutic relationships. Tauber reminded us how easy it is for psychotherapists to lose themselves in their clients, to merge—to sit in the client's chair, so to speak. Adopting an image of therapist and client, each in their own chair, can help to shed light on the dance of psychotherapy. When we are maintaining our professional distance, we are firmly planted in our own chairs. However, when we are succumbing to the impact from the feelings or states of our clients, it is as if we are no longer in our own chair. In those instances we have, in essence, moved over into the client's chair and are sitting there with him, experiencing what he is experiencing. From his chair, it is no longer possible to discriminate our own bodies and feelings, have a professional distance, or think clearly.

As demonstrated in the foregoing pages, this process can have deleterious consequences. To help her avoid, or at least greatly reduce, the risks of compassion fatigue, vicarious trauma, and burnout, the therapist must learn to stay in her own chair—that is, to feel her own body and her own emotions, and to limit the imagery and mirroring that would pull her into the client's chair. A periodic quick visit to the client's chair can be useful and give much-needed insight. However, to be able to adequately help our clients, we must remain in our own chair.

I've learned through several years of supervising and training psychotherapists that considering reducing resonance with their clients can seem threatening for some. Putting the concept into a continuum has been helpful for understanding that the goal is to be aware of what level of contact you choose, navigating between symbiosis on the one hand and separation on the other. Remember that you have many choices also in between. When you are together with a particular client, your range of contact should be changing periodically, with all points possible depending on what is needed at the time and what is optimal for your own well-being.

It is up to each reader—either on your own or with assistance from colleagues or a consultant—to discover which combinations of principles and strategies, from this volume and other sources, will best help you to stay in your own chair. You will probably need to experiment with several skills to find your own optimal mix. As an example, one successful combination of theory and tools is illustrated in the following case. (It has been published elsewhere in slightly altered forms [Rothschild, 2002a, 2002b].)* As you read this case, please remember that what works for Ruth is merely one possible mix of tools. Each of us needs to tailor our own individual strategy to take charge of managing our risks for compassion fatigue, vicarious trauma, and burnout.

Ruth is a clinical social worker in a family service agency. After a few months on a new job she was beginning to feel exhausted and depressed. In fact, she was so depleted, she was afraid she would have to quit her job and go on disability. Though she knew it was difficult counseling victims of disaster, she did not know what else to do. This was her chosen profession, her life's ambition. Usually it provided her with an intense feeling of satisfaction. She liked to bask in the success of helping desperate people using her talent for resolving stress and trauma. But now she feared she was speeding toward that dreaded therapist risk: burnout. Happy to be able to help others who were less fortunate than herself, Ruth felt lucky. She wanted to give thanks with her service. However, she was frustrated to think that she might have to cease the work that was so meaningful to her rather than risk her physical and mental health.

I was hired by Ruth's workplace as a consultant and supervisor. During a weekly meeting, she bravely revealed her predicament. The first thing I wanted to know was how long she had been feeling this way. To the best of her recollection, it was fairly recent, in the last few weeks. Her answer cued my next question: Were there any unusually difficult new

---

* This case study first appeared in: Rothschild (2002a), Case studies: The Dangers of Empathy. *Psychotherapy Networker, 16,* 4.

cases during that time? Yes, there were, and she proceeded to tell me about one particularly demanding case. As Ruth spoke about her new client, she began to show distinct signs of heightened stress arousal. She became very pale and broke out in a cold sweat. I could see that her hands were shaking slightly. I stopped her report and drew attention to her body responses. She named sensations that corresponded to what I had observed: she was cold, wet, and shaky. Tears came to her eyes. When I asked what she was feeling, she began to cry. "What is happening to me?" she asked. "I used to be able to handle much more than this!"

While Ruth's reaction was intense, it was not unusual. Working with traumatized people is demanding and wearing and can be upsetting. Some cases are easier to handle than others, but the need for self-care and self-protection is always pertinent. In each case, there are several areas worth exploring. Below, these are first accessed. In the last section, strategies for intervening and helping Ruth's difficulties are described.

Evaluating Risks for Vicarious Trauma

Three major areas of investigation are pertinent to Ruth's situation:

1. How she processes the information given by the client for clues to the source of her upset.
2. Assessing the interaction between Ruth and her client could be very useful. There might be something in the interaction itself that is having a negative impact on her.
3. In this instance, it seemed a good idea to look for any issues that may be personally provocative. This will not always be the case, but it is worth looking into.

PROCESSING CLIENT INFORMATION

I asked Ruth to tell me a little about this distressing case. As she described the details of her client's situation, I pe-

riodically stopped the narrative to ask Ruth what she was feeling, seeing, and hearing in her mind. She was able to answer easily. She was always accustomed to picturing a client's situation in her mind's eye, creating images of the client's life and struggles.   •

It became immediately clear that when Ruth pictured her client's situation, she was not an objective observer seeing the situation from the outside. Ruth tended to place herself in the client's perspective, in her shoes, and see the situation, as it were, through the client's eyes. From that angle, Ruth was also vulnerable to feeling a similar stress in her body and similar emotions. Though she was used to this method of gaining empathy with her clients, usually she was better able to separate the client's experience and feelings from her own. But in this case, Ruth's usual talent had failed her. To find out why and how, I needed to explore further.

OBSERVING THE INTERACTION

"How," I asked, "do you sit with your client? What is your interaction like when you are in your office engaged in helping the client?"

Ruth usually placed the client's chair close to her or at the side of her desk so that they could almost literally put their heads together at times. Ruth tended to lean toward the client and was accustomed to mimicking facial expressions and gestures as a way of communicating empathy. For example, when the client had a pained expression, Ruth would copy it on her own face. She wanted her clients to see that she was moved by their plight.

PERSONAL PROVOCATION

Finally, I asked Ruth to consider if anything in her client's situation reminded her of anything from her own personal history. That was a bit more difficult for Ruth to ad-

dress. She prided herself on her ability to be objective with her clients and not let her private life interfere. She was embarrassed to even consider that she might have let personal feelings intrude into her work.

No, she had never experienced anything like her client's situation. Nothing. I asked her to look more broadly, perhaps into the situation of someone close to her. Slowly the realization dawned on her. There were many parallels between her client's situation and something that had happened to an older cousin who had been Ruth's caretaker when she was a child. When the cousin got into trouble, Ruth had been too young to help her. The cousin had not received the help she had needed and had suffered grave consequences. Ruth had silently vowed to help others as she had not been able to help her cousin. In fact, Ruth realized, her fervor for her profession had roots in her cousin's misfortune.

Reversing the Effects of Vicarious Trauma -

In Ruth's case, the keys to her vicarious trauma and burnout emerged quite clearly. This is not always the case, but often at least one category of vulnerability will be visible. Over three supervision sessions, Ruth was helped to identify and rectify the source of her vicarious trauma. The details of the strategies Ruth found helpful in each area are outlined below.

LIMITING IMAGERY, -

It is not necessary to picture a client's situation to understand it. In fact, sometimes—as in Ruth's case—producing traumatic pictures in the mind's eye can be very upsetting. Ruth needed to learn how to listen to her client, letting the words communicate the situation. I suggested that Ruth experiment with varying her way of being with her client. She could try sometimes to attend only to words, and sometimes rely on her usual mode of creating images. She might also experiment with creating images from different angles: from the client's perspective, from an observer's perspective, an aerial view, and so forth. The idea was to give Ruth more control over how she received and processed information. I suggested she keep a record of which strategy she was using and to evaluate each according to her somatic and emotional responses after the client left. Such investigation should eventually lead Ruth to a kind of empathy that would not debilitate her.

PROXIMITY MAY MATTER

While necessary to the helping professions, what comprises empathy is often misconstrued. Understanding someone's pain is not the same as feeling it. The former is needed for helping, but the latter can hinder it.

> *The interaction between Ruth and her client in the office exacerbated what the imagery had started. In such close proximity, mimicking gestures and expressions, Ruth came to feel nearly exactly what her client was feeling: depressed and desperate. The difficulty with this is common sense. It is not possible to help a desperate person if the therapist is herself feeling desperate. One person in the room must be able to maintain objectivity to be able to identify and engage helpful action. A desperate client is not capable of this, so it is up to the therapist to establish enough separation to maintain her ability to help.*
>
> *Again, experimentation was in order. Ruth was encouraged to practice mindfulness, paying particular attention to her body sensations and facial expressions. She discovered that she needed to practice facial expressions that would communicate concern without leaving her vulnerable to catching every emotion the client was feeling. Ruth came to the conclusion that she needed greater distance between the client and herself. She moved the client's chair across the desk from her own, instead of at the side. The desk, Ruth felt, provided a natural boundary that protected her, to some degree, from feeling so much of her client's pain. She also set out to learn to iden-*

tify when she was mimicking her client's facial expres-
sion. When she noticed this, she found that sitting back
in her chair and taking a deep breath cut the flow of client
emotion into her own body. Much to her surprise, though,
it did not diminish her ability to be empathetic. Actually,
she found her ability to help increase proportionately.

HEALING OLD PAIN

For most of us, our own history impacts greatly on our choice
of career. This is a huge benefit, but it can also be a deficit if
we try to delude ourselves about our motivations and if we do
not keep our perspective clear.

Finally, Ruth had to take a deeper look at the impact of her
cousin's trauma. It was necessary for Ruth to separate the
client's situation from her cousin's, to be able to see that
nothing like her cousin's trouble threatened Ruth now.
With the aid of supervision, Ruth could maintain intel-
lectual awareness of the difference. For a deeper healing
of this issue, she determined to seek counseling herself.

Compassion fatigue and vicarious trauma can be healed
and even prevented when the mechanisms leading to them
are identified and made conscious. Once vulnerabilities are
assessed, strategies for increasing awareness and control can
be instituted. Experimentation and evaluation are the keys
to helping each therapist discover which interventions are
most effective for keeping her in her own chair.

FINAL WORDS

[A]utomatic empathy has all the [force] of running or tumbling
downhill, controlled empathy is as effortful as climbing up a
mountainside.

—*Hodges & Wegner* (1997, p. 320)

We all know that empathy is the connective tissue of good therapy. It facilitates the development of trust in our clients and allows us to meet them with our feelings as well as our thoughts. Empathy also hones our tools of insight and intuition, and complements our theoretical knowledge. But when the mechanisms of empathy are not in our awareness or under our control, we can find ourselves in real trouble.

In the forgoing pages, I have strived to shed light on the neurological, psychological, and somatic mechanisms by which this gift, our capacity for empathy, can turn back on us with a vengeance. Without mastery of our own talents and tendencies toward empathy, it can mutate, twisting our compassion into compassion fatigue and our resonance into vicarious traumatization. It is my hope that the theory, insights, and skills offered here have helped you to better manage your empathy for the benefit of both yourself and your clients.

APPENDICES

Appendix 1

Assessment

Rigorous assessment for compassion fatigue, vicarious traumatization, and burnout is difficult. There are several tests and scales that attempt to measure these conditions, but none is foolproof, nor yet substantiated. Results of any of these or other tests can be skewed or have a bias. Therefore, it is recommended that you use these scales only as a guideline in assessing your own situation. Where available, relevant comments by a scale's author are indicated.

Keep in mind that the best indicator for evaluating if you are suffering from your work in any way is not a scale, but you: your own body and mind. Pay attention to your body awareness and self-awareness, as discussed throughout this volume. Those will be your very best tools. And *use your common sense*. Here are three examples. If you are feeling poorly in some way following every session with the same client, look for clues to the difficulties you may be having with that client and what he is working on. When you are disconcerted following a particular session, review what happened there. If you have a more general feeling of discord that pervades your private life daily, you may need to look at your overall work situation, your family, or even personal history or development issues. And don't forget to pay attention to the obvious: A recent spat with your partner, a cold coming on, hormonal fluctuations, etc.

As mentioned in the introduction, this book focuses on the therapeutic relationship. However, this appendix includes two instruments that may be suited to evaluate stressors from other areas of your life as well. Again, though, use your common sense. If a close family member is seriously ill, you do not need a psychological instrument to tell you that you are under stress and that such a situation could affect your health and your work. On the other hand, if you are the type of person who tends to deny the impact of stressful events on you, some of these tests—or others you find—maybe useful for you.

The bottom line: Know yourself as well as you can. Take a personal inventory using the body awareness, self-awareness, and personal history tools from this book (and others that are helpful to you). Get a baseline for what is usual for you so you will know when you have ventured away from your own norm. Listen to the feedback of colleagues, family, and friends. If they are telling you that you look tired, are acting irritable, seem depressed, or are behaving in a manic way, take notice. You will never know if you agree or disagree unless you take their feedback seriously and consider it. Lastly, remember, you are the best expert on yourself—better still when you pay attention.

ProQOL-R IV*

PROFESSIONAL QUALITY OF LIFE SCALE
COMPASSION SATISFACTION AND FATIGUE
SUBSCALES—REVISION IV

[Helping] people puts you in direct contact with their lives. As you probably have experienced, your compassion for those you [help] has both positive and negative aspects. We would like to ask you questions about your experiences, both positive and negative, as a [helper]. Consider each of the following questions about you and your current situation. Select the number that honestly reflects how frequently you experienced these characteristics in the *last 30 days*.

| 0 = Never | 2 = A Few Times | 4 = Often |
| 1 = Rarely | 3 = Somewhat Often | 5 = Very Often |

_____ 1. I am happy.

_____ 2. I am preoccupied with more than one person I [help].

_____ 3. I get satisfaction from being able to [help] people.

_____ 4. I feel connected to others.

_____ 5. I jump or am startled by unexpected sounds.

_____ 6. I feel invigorated after working with those I [help].

_____ 7. I find it difficult to separate my personal life from my life as a [helper].

_____ 8. I am losing sleep over traumatic experiences of a person I [help].

_____ 9. I think that I might have been "infected" by the traumatic stress of those I [help].

_____10. I feel trapped by my work as a [helper].

_____11. Because of my [helping], I have felt "on edge" about various things.

_____12. I like my work as a [helper].

_____13. I feel depressed as a result of my work as a [helper].

* Scales and self-scoring directions reprinted by permission of Beth Stamm. © B. Hudnall Stamm, 1997–2005. *Professional Quality of Life: Compassion Satisfaction and Fatigue Subscales, R-IV (ProQOL).* http://www.isu.edu/~bhstamm. This test may be freely copied as long as (a) author is credited, (b) no changes are made, and (c) it is not sold. This information is presented for educational purposes only. It is not a substitute for informed medical advice or training. Do not use this information to diagnose or treat a health problem without consulting a qualified health or mental health care provider. If you have concerns, contact your health care provider, mental health professional, or your community health center.

_____14. I feel as though I am experiencing the trauma of someone I have [helped].

_____15. I have beliefs that sustain me.

_____16. I am pleased with how I am able to keep up with [helping] techniques and protocols.

_____17. I am the person I always wanted to be.

_____18. My work makes me feel satisfied.

_____19. Because of my work as a [helper], I feel exhausted.

_____20. I have happy thoughts and feelings about those I [help] and how I could help them.

_____21. I feel overwhelmed by the amount of work or the size of my case[work]load I have to deal with.

_____22. I believe I can make a difference through my work.

_____23. I avoid certain activities or situations because they remind me of frightening experiences of the people I [help].

_____24. I am proud of what I can do to [help].

_____25. As a result of my [helping], I have intrusive, frightening thoughts.

_____26. I feel "bogged down" by the system.

_____27. I have thoughts that I am a "success" as a [helper].

_____28. I can't recall important parts of my work with trauma victims.

_____29. I am a very sensitive person.

_____30. I am happy that I chose to do this work.

Self-scoring directions, if used as self-test

1. Be certain you respond to all items.

2. On some items the scores need to be reversed. Next to your response write the reverse of that score (i.e., 0=0, 1=5, 2=4, 3=3). Reverse the scores on these 5 items: 1, 4, 15, 17 and 29. Please note that the value 0 is not reversed, as its value is always null.

3. Mark the items for scoring:
   a. Put an **X** by the 10 items that form the **Compassion Satisfaction Scale**: 3, 6, 12, 16, 18, 20, 22, 24, 27, 30.
   b. Put a **check** by the 10 items on the **Burnout Scale**: 1, 4, 8, 10, 15, 17, 19, 21, 26, 29.
   c. **Circle** the 10 items on the **Trauma/Compassion Fatigue Scale**: 2, 5, 7, 9, 11, 13, 14, 23, 25, 28.

4. Add the numbers you wrote next to the items for each set of items and compare with the theoretical scores.

Note: You may substitute the appropriate target group for *[helper]* if that is not the best term. For example, if you are working with teachers, replace *[helper]* with teacher. Word changes may be made to any word in italicized square brackets to make the measure read more smoothly for a particular target group.

YOUR SCORES ON THE ProQOL: PROFESSIONAL QUALITY OF LIFE SCREENING

Based on your responses, your personal scores are below. If you have any concerns, you should discuss them with a physical or mental health care professional.

Compassion Satisfaction _____

Compassion satisfaction is about the pleasure you derive from being able to do your work well. For example, you may feel like it is a pleasure to help others through your work. You may feel positively about your colleagues or your ability to contribute to the work setting or even the greater good of society. Higher scores on this scale represent a greater satisfaction related to your ability to be an effective caregiver in your job.

The average score is 37 (SD 7; alpha scale reliability .87). About 25% of people score higher than 42 and about 25% of people score below 33. If you are in the higher range, you probably derive a good deal of professional satisfaction from your position. If your scores are below 33, you may either find problems with your job, or there may be some other reason—for example, you might derive your satisfaction from activities other than your job.

Burnout_____

Most people have an intuitive idea of what burnout is. From the research perspective, burnout is associated with feelings of hopelessness and difficulties in dealing with work or in doing your job effectively. These negative feelings usually have a gradual onset. They can reflect the feeling that your efforts make no difference, or they can be associated with a very high workload or a non-supportive work environment. Higher scores on this scale mean that you are at higher risk for burnout.

The average score on the burnout scale is 22 (SD 6.0; alpha scale reliability .72). About 25% of people score above 27 and about 25% of people score below 18. If your score is below 18, this probably reflects positive feelings about your ability to be effective in your work. If you score above 27 you may wish to think about what at work makes you feel like you are not effective in your position. Your score may reflect your mood; perhaps you were having a "bad day" or are in need of some time off. If the high score persists or if it is reflective of other worries, it may be a cause for concern.

Compassion Fatigue/Secondary Trauma_____

Compassion fatigue (CF), also called secondary trauma (STS) and related to Vicarious Trauma (VT), is about your work-related, secondary exposure to extremely stressful events. For example, you may repeatedly hear stories about the traumatic things that happen to other people, commonly called VT. If your work puts you directly in the path of danger, such as being a soldier or humanitarian aide worker, this is not secondary exposure; your exposure is primary. However, if you are exposed to others' traumatic events as a result of your work, such as in an emergency room or working with child protective services, this is secondary exposure. The symptoms of CF/STS are usually rapid in onset and associated with a particular event. They may include being afraid, having difficulty sleeping, having images of the upsetting event pop into your mind, or avoiding things that remind you of the event.

The average score on this scale is 13 (SD 6; alpha scale reliability .80). About 25% of people score below 8 and about 25% of people score above 17. If your score is above 17, you may want to take some time to think about what at work may be frightening to you or if there is some other reason for the elevated score. While higher scores do not mean that you do have a problem, they are an indication that you may want to examine how you feel about your work and your work environment. You may wish to discuss this with your supervisor, a colleague, or a health care professional.

WORLD ASSUMPTIONS SCALE*

Using the scale below, please select the number that indicates how much you agree or disagree with each statement. Please answer honestly. Thanks.

1.	2.	3.	4.	5.	6.
strongly disagree	moderately disagree	slightly disagree	slightly agree	moderately agree	strongly agree

1.___ Misfortune is least likely to strike worthy, decent people.
2.___ People are naturally unfriendly and unkind.[a]
3.___ Bad events are distributed to people at random.[a]
4.___ Human nature is basically good.
5.___ The good things that happen in this world far outnumber the bad.
6.___ The course of our lives is largely determined by chance.[a]
7.___ Generally, people deserve what they get in this world.
8.___ I often think I am no good at all. [a]
9.___ There is more good than evil in the world.
10.___ I am basically a lucky person.
11.___ People's misfortunes result from mistakes they have made.
12.___ People don't really care what happens to the next person.[a]
13.___ I usually behave in ways that are likely to maximize good results for me.
14.___ People will experience good fortune if they themselves are good.
15.___ Life is too full of uncertainties that are determined by chance. [a]
16.___ When I think about it, I consider myself very lucky.
17.___ I almost always make an effort to prevent bad things from happening to me.
18.___ I have a low opinion of myself.[a]
19.___ By and large, good people get what they deserve in this world.
20.___ Through our actions we can prevent bad things from happening to us.
21.___ Looking at my life, I realize that chance events have worked out well for me.
22.___ If people took preventive actions, most misfortune could be avoided.
23.___ I take the actions necessary to protect myself against misfortune.
24.___ In general, life is mostly a gamble.[a]
25.___ The world is a good place.
26.___ People are basically kind and helpful.
27.___ I usually behave so as to bring about the greatest good for me.
28.___ I am very satisfied with the kind of person I am.
29.___ When bad things happen, it is typically because people have not taken the necessary actions to protect themselves.
30.___ If you look closely enough, you will see that the world is full of goodness.
31.___ I have reason to be ashamed of my personal character.[a]
32.___ I am luckier than most people.

[a] reverse score

Scoring

Reverse score the statements noted [a] and then sum the responses for each of the three subscales, as indicated below.

Benevolence of the World: items 2 + 4 + 5 + 9 + 12 + 25 + 26 + 30
Meaningfulness of the World: items 1+3 + 6 + 7 + 11 + 14 + 15 + 19 + 20 + 22 + 24 + 29
Self-Worth: items 8 + 10 + 13 + 16 + 17 + 18 + 21 + 23 + 27 + 28 + 31 + 32

SOCIAL READJUSTMENT RATING SCALE: STRESSFUL LIFE EVENTS*

Note: May be used to evaluate your general level of life stress

Life Events	Score
Death of spouse	100
Divorce	73
Marital separation from mate	65
Detention in jail, other institution	63
Death of a close family member	63
Major personal injury or illness	53
Marriage	50
Fired from work	47
Marital reconciliation	45
Retirement	45
Major change in the health or behavior of a family member	44
Pregnancy	40
Sexual difficulties	39
Gaining a new family member (e.g., through birth, adoption, oldster moving, etc.)	39
Major business readjustment (e.g., merger, reorganization, bankruptcy)	39
Major change in financial status	38
Death of close friend	37
Change to different line of work	36
Major change in the number of arguments with spouse	35
Taking out a mortgage or loan for a major purchase	31
Foreclosure on a mortgage or loan	30
Major change in responsibilities at work	29
Son or daughter leaving home (e.g., marriage, attending college)	29
Trouble with in-laws	29
Outstanding personal achievement	28

* T. H. Holmes and R. H. Rahe (1967). The social adjustment rating scale. *Journal of Psychosomatic Research 2(1)*, 213–218. © 1967 Elsevier, Inc. Reprinted by permission of Elsevier, Inc.

Spouse beginning or ceasing to work outside the home	26
Beginning or ceasing formal schooling	26
Major change in living conditions	25
Revision of personal habits (dress, manners, associations, etc.)	24
Trouble with boss	23
Major change in working hours or conditions	20
Change in residence	20
Change to a new school	20
Major change in usual type and/or amount of recreation	19
Major change in church activities (a lot more or less than usual)	19
Major change in social activities (clubs, dancing, movies, visiting)	18
Taking out a mortgage or loan for a lesser purchase (e.g., for a car, TV, freezer, etc.)	17
Major change in sleeping habits	16
Major change in the number of family get-togethers	15
Major change in eating habits	15
Vacation	13
Christmas season	12
Minor violations of the law (e.g., traffic tickets, etc.)	11
Total	___

Add up your score. The higher the total, the more stress you are under. Scores of 150 and higher increase risk for illness.

PTSD CHECKLIST CIVILIAN VERSION (PCL)*

Note: May be used to evaluate your level of vicarious trauma

Instructions: Below is a list of problems and complaints that people sometimes have in response to stressful experiences. Please read each one carefully, and put an X in the box to indicate how much you have been bothered by that problem *in the past month.*

Response	Not at all (1)	A little bit (2)	Moderately (3)	Quite a bit (4)	Extremely (5)
1. Repeated, disturbing *memories, thoughts, or images* of a stressful experience from the past?					
2. Repeated, disturbing *dreams* of a stressful experience from the past?					
3. Suddenly *acting* or *feeling* as if a stressful experience *were happening* again (as if you were reliving it)?					
4. Feeling *very upset* when *something reminded* you of a stressful experience from the past?					
5. Having *physical reactions* (e.g., heart pounding, trouble breathing, or sweating) when *something reminded* you of a stressful experience from the past?					
6. Avoid *thinking about* or *talking about* a stressful experience from the past or avoid *having feelings* related to it?					
7. Avoid *activities* or *situations* because they *remind you* of a stressful experience from the past?					
8. Trouble *remembering important parts* of a stressful experience from the past?					
9. Loss of *interest in things that you used to enjoy?*					
10. Feeling *distant* or *cut off* from other people?					
11. Feeling *emotionally numb* or being unable to have loving feelings for those close to you?					
12. Feeling as if your *future* will somehow be *cut short?*					
13. Trouble *falling* or *staying asleep?*					
14. Feeling *irritable* or having *angry outbursts?*					
15. Having *difficulty concentrating?*					
16. Being *"super alert"* or watchful on guard?					
17. Feeling *jumpy* or easily startled?					

Here are a few references on the PCL. These were taken from the PILOTS database (the world's largest database on traumatic stress) http://www.ncptsd. org/PILOTS.html. There are other citations of the PCL, which has been used in hundreds of studies. Please consult PILOTS for more information.

Smith, M. Y., Redd, W. H., DuHamel, K., Vickberg, S. J., & Ricketts, P. (1999). Validation of the PTSD Checklist-Civilian version in survivors of bone marrow transplantation. *Journal of Traumatic Stress, 12*(3), 485–499.

Campbell, K. A., Rohlman, D. S., Storzbach, D., Binder, L. M., Anger, W. K., Kovera, C. A., et al. (1999). Test-retest reliability of psychological and neurobehavioral tests self-administered by computer. *Assessment, 6*(1), 21–32.

Manne, S. L., Du Hamel, K., Gallelli, K., Sorgen, K., & Redd, W. H. (1998). Posttraumatic stress disorder among mothers of pediatric cancer survivors: Diagnosis, comorbidity, and utility of the PTSD Checklist as a screening instrument. *Journal of Pediatric Psychology, 23*(6), 357–366.

Andrykowski, M. A., Cordova, M. J., Studts, J. L., & Miller, T. W. (1998). Posttraumatic stress disorder after treatment for breast cancer: Prevalence of diagnosis and use of the PTSD Checklist–Civilian Version (PCL-C) as a screening instrument. *Journal of Consulting and Clinical Psychology, 66*(3), 586–590.

Blanchard, E. B., Jones-Alexander, J., Buckley, T. C., & Forneris, C. A. (1996). Psychometric properties of the PTSD Checklist (PCL). *Behaviour Research and Therapy, 34*(8), 669–673.

Koivisto, H., & Haapasalo, J. (1996). Childhood maltreatment and adulthood psychopathology in light of file-based assessments among mental state examinees. *Studies on Crime and Crime Prevention, 5*(1), 91–104.

Cordova, M. J., Andrykowski, M. A., Kenady, D. E., McGrath, P. C., Sloan, D. A., & Redd, W. H. (1995). Frequency and correlates of posttraumatic-stress-disorder-like symptoms after treatment for breast cancer. *Journal of Consulting and Clinical Psychology, 63*(6), 981–986.

LIFE STATUS REVIEW*

Instructions: Mark one box for each item listed within the eight categories below, based on your current situation. Marking "0" indicates things are functional, but could be much better or could be much worse. A "−1" or "−2" indicates that you are experiencing difficulties in these areas of your life. A "+1" or "+2" indicates that you are experiencing success or have had no problems in these areas of your life.

Patient Number_____ Location #_____
Date_____ Clinician_____

	Serious* −2	An Issue −1	Fine 0	Good +1	Great +2
Medical					
health					
medication					
hospitalization					
Health/Wellness					
exercise					
rest/relaxation					
nutrition/access to food					
Financial					
debts					
income					
SSI/Disability/Assistance					
Housing/Transportation					
apartment/home					
access to shops, services					
environmental conditions					
access to transportation					
Employment/School					
stability					
working conditions					
relationships at work/school					

	Serious* −2	An Issue −1	Fine 0	Good +1	Great +2
Legal/Criminal					
civil					
family					
criminal					
parole/probation					
Alcohol/Substance Use					
other's complaining					
arrested/hospitalized					
problems related to use					
Self/Social/Interpersonal					
family relations					
intimate relations					
spirituality/belief systems					
children's health & well-being					
friend/family communication					
organizations (club, religious group)					
Other					

Pilot Research

Over the past few years, along with colleagues Maggie Shiffrar, Ph.D., at Rutgers University in New Jersey and Emerald Jane Turner, M.A., at London Transport in the UK, I have directed three pilot research projects. At this point, we have mostly raw data from rather small samples. However, descriptions of the projects and our preliminary findings are very pertinent to this book. Readers are cautioned to regard this material as completely preliminary. Nonetheless, it is hoped that you will find interest and value in their inclusion. Further, anyone wishing to conduct similar studies is welcome to contact me for consultation.

RESEARCH PROJECT I:
POSTURAL MIRRORING
AND SOMATIC EMPATHY

One of these experiments was already described in Chapter 2. For convenience, it is reproduced here, followed by a discussion of this and other similar experiments.

During a pilot study conducted in 2003 (Rothschild &
Shiffrar, 2003, 2004) as part of a training course in Eu-

rope, I asked one of the group sponsors to silently model his posture after something reminiscent of an emotional situation from his life and to hold it steady for a few minutes. He struck a pose with one arm elevated behind him, the other reaching outward and down in front of him; his feet were about a foot and a half apart, placed one in front of the other; his torso bent slightly forward.

No words or verbal information of any kind were communicated to the group members. Half of the group was instructed to copy his posture, the other half just to observe it. Following the exercise, the group members filled out questionnaires indicating the physical sensations, feelings, thoughts, and images they experienced, and to guess what the model may have been remembering. After the group members had a chance to note their personal responses and fill out their questionnaires, the sponsor was allowed to speak. He told us that he had remembered being a teenager, saving a younger sibling from drowning in a stream in the woods.

The responses to the questionnaires from the mirroring half of the group were fascinating. No one had known what the situation was—none had somatic markers for anything similar. However, several in that half felt a powerful effort or struggle in their own bodies and a sense of urgency. Generally they reported feeling strong and focused. Fear was the predominant emotion. Some had visual images of being outdoors and of water or trees.

Considering that the remembered scenario was something totally outside of the average person's experience, the results were quite astonishing. With the same group, another sponsor had modeled a posture that would be quite familiar to almost anyone (i.e., most would have somatic markers for it); feeding her infant grandchild. The results were intriguing. Among both the mirroring and the observing halves, there was an extremely high correlation of sensations, emotions, and images. In addition, the majority easily guessed that the situation had something to do with caring for a young child. Likely, these higher cor-

relations could be predicted since just about every adult has somatic markers for caring for a baby.

The set of pilot studies of which the one above is part began a long time ago as the mirroring exercise that appears in Chapter 2. For many years I have informally used this exercise during 12-day professional training programs (and actually still do). It is very useful in helping the professional participants to understand somatic empathy. The results were always astounding but were never documented. When this book began to take shape, the idea to formally use that exercise to obtain hard data was born. I approached Maggie Shiffrar, a professor at Rutgers University who specializes in the study of movement recognition. We had been corresponding about her work for a while. Together we drafted feedback forms. Several pilot studies were conducted using these forms, including one with a group of nearly 200. Those early attempts were disastrous, and we learned to simplify our forms and drastically reduce our sample size.

There were 16 participants in the European sample described above. The group was divided in half. For each of the two runs, half of the group precisely mimicked (mirrored) the posture and other half merely observed it, not changing their own posture in any way. For the second run-through, we reversed the groups, letting the previous "mirrors" now be "observers," and vice versa. In the end, each subject tried being both a mirror and an observer.

Even the observers accurately guessed the theme of the second model's posture. We suspect that is because caring for a young child is within just about everyone's experience. However, emotions and body sensations were not shared as strongly in the observer group as in the mirror group.

The experience with the first model was different. He was remembering something outside of usual experience. Observers were totally at a loss for any kind of matching. The empathy of the mirrors was much weaker than with the second model, but still there were significant resonances.

Our major problem with this series of studies is in refining the feedback instrument to rule out confounding factors. We are still at it (as much as bicoastal collaboration allows) and hope to have more rigorous data available soon.

RESEARCH PROJECT II:
APPLICATIONS OF MIRRORING AND
UNMIRRORING IN PRACTICE

We have only had one trial. The goal of this study (Rothschild et al., 2005) was to determine if adding both theory and tools for mirroring and unmirroring would decrease vulnerability to vicarious trauma and burnout in a group of professional psychotherapists.

I directed the project and Emerald Jane Turner, a supervisor for an agency that primarily treats traumatized clients, conducted it. Maggie Shiffrar was our research consultant. (All three of us have successfully completed the Rutgers University Human Subjects Compliance Program.) Turner was responsible for the supervision of 12 practitioners, 9 of whom agreed to participate in this study. We realized from the start that this was a very small sample—4 in the experimental group and 5 in the control group—but it was a good place to start. Each group received the same biweekly individual supervision as always. The experimental group received, in addition, instruction in body awareness, postural mirroring, and unmirroring. We pretested, posttested, and posttested at 3 months using the Compassion Fatigue Test (Figley & Stamm, 1996), Maslach Burnout Inventory: Human Services Survey (Maslach & Jackson, 1986), and the World Assumptions Scale (Janoff-Bulmann, 1996).

Over the duration of the study, which lasted several months, two dropped from the control group and one from the experimental group. In the end, there were just three in each group. The reasons for dropout point up some of the difficulties in conducting studies on vicarious trauma: One subject left the agency due to administrative restructuring; one had extended personal leave due to family illness; and the third was absent for an extended period of time due to surgery and convalescence. Also, during this time the agency moved and a new director was appointed; both events greatly affected all of the staff. Of those participating in the study, two lost close family members and another was witness to a tragic incident. Turner reports that all of these factors made it difficult to keep supervision sessions focused on work with clients, let alone trying to teach new theory and tools. She suggested that testing the same hypothesis may be easier with a group of therapists in private practice. At least then the skewing due to agency issues would be absent.

Despite the small number of participants, preliminary analysis of this project's data is encouraging: There was a 25% reduction in burnout scores in the experimental group. We would like to see this study conducted with a larger agency. If any reader thinks her agency would like to participate, please contact me (per info on the copyright page).

RESEARCH PROJECT III:
PILOT HELP FOR THE HELPER
TRAINING COURSE

In October 2004, I conducted the first 4-day professional training utilizing the theory and skills of this book (Rothschild & Shiffrar, 2004). The course included lectures on the theory, practice in the skills and exercises, and individual consultation sessions for those who desired them (in much the same style as some of the transcripts in the text). I regret that I did not pretest the participants. However, a few months following the course, I polled them for their feedback. Using a typical 1–10 scale, I asked the group about levels of stress before and following the course, and what kind of impact the course had had on their professional lives. Of course, the investigative format was much too loose to count as hard data. Nonetheless, the results are useful and have provided me both with encouragement and with ammunition to further refine the course. Basically, everyone found some aspect of the course useful for their professional lives. A majority found many aspects useful. Attendance was kept small to allow time for individual attention. In all, 14 professionals participated over the 4 days of the course.

All but two of those attending had come to the course with stress levels of 5 or higher; half were at 7 and up. Two thirds of the group had significant drops in stress over the first week following the course, and all but one maintained lower stress levels at the time of the poll. One participant had an initial increase in stress due to increased awareness of workplace problems, but the stress decreased when she was able to apply skills learned in the course. All but two found the course meaningful for improving their work situation and none thought it worsened their job stress.

The following is a list of skills and interventions individuals found particularly useful and are still using:

1. Remembering to ask myself how I need to look after myself with each client.
2. Being mindful of clients "hitching a ride" home with me at the end of the day.
3. Paying attention to how I dress with clients.
4. Being aware that I have a choice in how much my client's feelings do or do not impact me.
5. Realizing how much stress I was absorbing through my eyes and taking steps to push that away now.
6. Paying attention to mirroring and unmirroring.
7. Maintaining a feel for my edges (skin boundaries).
8. I've become better at judging when I need to lower my arousal, and when it is better for me to stay with and contain it.
9. A good session doesn't have to mean that I must suffer along with my client.

10. I'm now more efficient without losing empathy.
11. Increasing my armor through muscle strengthening on a daily basis.
12. Having more choices for how to be with my client.

Acknowledgments

Every book owes its existence to more than the credited author or authors. That is certainly the case with this volume; many have assisted with its gestation, labor, and birth. I would like to thank all who gave ideas, wisdom, criticism, and support. Hopefully, I will remember you all, but if one or two of you slip past me in a "senior moment," please forgive me and remind me for future printings.

First, I would like to recognize Marjorie Rand, Ph.D., for her contributions to the first draft of this book, particularly the sections Countertransference, Projective Identification, Revisiting Projective Identification, and Empathy. Despite multiple revisions, many of her thoughts remain.

Innumerable professionals—supervisors, teachers, colleagues, students, and supervisees—have inspired the creation of this book. Your shared experiences have been instrumental in shaping these ideas and helping me to explain them cogently.

Many, many thanks go to colleagues who read earlier versions of this manuscript and dared to offer their brutally honest opinions: John May, Ph.D., Bonnita Wirth, Ph.D., Sima Rae Stanley, MSW, Vicki Salvin, MSW, Maggie Shiffrar, Ph.D., Phoebus Tongas, Ph.D., Alan Karbling, Ph.D., Yvonne Tauber, Ph.D., Ellert Nijenhuis, Ph.D., and Marion Solomon, Ph.D.

Much appreciation goes to Charles Figley, Ph.D., who coined the term *compassion fatigue* as the title of his 1995 book. He graciously gave permission to use his term in the subtitle of this volume.

Special thanks are extended to pioneer Elaine Hatfield, Ph.D. Her book, *Emotional Contagion*, inspired several of the ideas in this volume.

Last, I would like to give many, many accolades to everyone at the Professional Books division of W.W. Norton—in both the New York and London offices. Per usual, all have extended help and support generously, thoroughly spoiling me for any other publisher. And special thanks to my editor, Deborah Malmud: Your savvy, common sense, warmth, and good humor have helped me through some very rough times. This book would not have made it to press without you!

References

Adolphs, R., Damasio, H., Tranel, D., Cooper, G., & Damasio, A. R. (2000). A role for somatosensory cortices in the visual recognition of emotion as revealed by three dimentional lesion mapping. *Journal of Neuroscience, 20*, 2683–2690.

Allport, F. (1924). *Social psychology.* Boston: Houghton Mifflin.

American Psychiatric Association. (1994). *Diagnostic and statistical manual of mental disorders* (4th ed.). Washington, DC: Author.

Andreas, A., & Andreas, T. (1987). *Change your mind and keep the change: Advanced NLP submodalities interventions.* Moab, UT: Real People Press.

Arbib, M. A., Billard, A., & Iacoboni, M. (2000). Synthetic brain imaging: Grasping, mirror neurons and imitation. *Neural Networks, 13*(8–9), 975–997.

Ax, A. A. (1964). Goals and methods of psychophysiology. *Psychophysiology, 1*, 8–25.

Bandler, R. (1985). *Using your brain—for a change.* Moab, UT: Real People Press.

Bandura, A., Ross, D., & Ross, S. A. (1963). Imitation of film-mediated aggressive models. *Journal of Abnormal and Social Psychology, 66*(1), 3–11.

Benjamin, L. R., & Benjamin, R. (1994). A group for partners and parents of MPD clients: I. Process and format. *Dissociation: Progress in the Dissociative Disorders, 7*(1), 35–43.

Bion, W. (1959). Attacks on linking. *International Journal of Psychoanalysis, 40*, 308–315

Blairy, S., Herrera, P., & Hess, U. (1999). Mimicry and the judgment of emotional facial expressions. *Journal of Nonverbal Behavior, 23*(1), 5–41.

Bodynamic Institute. Bodynamic Institute Training Program, 1988–1992, Copenhagen, Denmark.

Bremner, J. D., Southwick, S., Brett, E., Fontana, A., Rosenheck, R., & Charney, D. S. (1992). Dissociation and posttraumatic stress disorder in Vietnam combat veterans. *American Journal of Psychiatry, 149*, 328–332.

Cannon, W. B. (1929). *Bodily changes in pain, anger, fear and rage, on account of recent researches into the function of emotional excitement* (2nd ed.). New York: Appleton.

Chartrand, T. I., & Bargh, J. A. (1999). The chameleon effect: The perception-behavior link and social interaction. *Journal of Personality and Social Psychology, 76,* 893–910.

Chollet, F., DiPiero, V., Wise, R. J., Brooks, D. J., Dolan, R. J., & Frackowiak, R. S. (1991). The functional anatomy of motor recovery after stroke in humans: A study with positron emission tomography. *Annals of Neurology, 29,* 63–71.

Classen, C., Koopman, C., & Spiegel, D. (1993). Trauma and dissociation. *Bulletin of the Menninger Clinic, 57*(2), 178–194.

Coleman, R. M., Greenblatt, M., & Solomon, H. (1956). Physiological evidence of rapport during psychotherapeutic interviews. *Diseases of the Nervous System, 17,* 71–77.

Cozolino, L. (2002). *The neuroscience of psychotherapy: Building and rebuilding the human brain.* New York: Norton.

Damasio, A. R. (1994). *Descartes' error.* New York: Putnam's Sons.

Damasio A. R. (1999). *The feeling of what happens: Body and emotion in the making of consciousness.* New York: Harcourt Brace.

Damasio, A. R. (2003). *Looking for Spinoza.* New York: Harcourt.

Darwin, C. (1965). *The expression of the emotions in man and animals.* Chicago: University of Chicago Press. (Original work published 1872).

Decety, J., & Chaminade, T. (2003). Neural correlates of feeling sympathy. *Neuropsychologia, 41,* 127–138.

DiMascio, A., Boyd, R. W., & Greenblatt, M. (1957). Physiological correlates of tension and antagonism during psychotherapy: A study of "interpersonal physiology." *Psychosomatic Medicine, 19,* 99–104.

DiMascio, A., Boyd, R. W., Greenblatt, M., & Solomon, H. C. (1955). The psychiatric interview: A sociophysiologic study. *Diseases of the Nervous System, 16,* 4–9.

Dimberg, U. (1982). Facial reactions to facial expressions. *Psychophysiology, 19,* 643–647.

Dimberg, U., Thunberg, M., & Elmehed, K. (2000). Unconscious facial reactions to emotional facial expressions. *Psychological Science, 11*(1), 86–89.

Doherty, R. W., Orimoto, L., Singelis, T. M., Hatfield, E., & Hebb, J. (1995). Emotional contagion: Gender and occupational differences. *Psychology of Women Quarterly, 19*(3), 355–371.

Duclos, S. E., Laird, J. D., Schneider, E., Sexter, M., Stern, L., & Van Lighten, O. (1989). Emotion-specific effects of facial expressions and postures on emotional experience.*Journal of Personality and Social Psychology, 57,* 100–108.

Ekman, P. (2003). *Emotions revealed: Recognizing faces and feelings to improve communication and emotional life.* New York: TimesBooks.

Ekman, P., Levenson, R. W., & Friesen, W. V. (1983). Autonomic nervous system activity distinguishes among emotions. *Science, 221,* 1208–1210.

Fadiga, L., Fogassi, L., Pavesi, G., & Rizzolatti, G. (1995). Motor facilitation during action observation: A magnetic stimulation study. *Journal of Neurophysiology, 73*(6), 2608–2611.

Figley, C. R. (1995). *Compassion fatigue: Coping with secondary traumatic stress disorder in those who treat the traumatized.* New York: Brunner/Mazel.

Figley, C. R., & Stamm, B. H. (1996). Psychometric view of Compassion Fatigue Self Test. In B. H. Stamm (Ed.), *Measurement of stress, trauma, and adaptation.* Lutherville, MD: Sidran Press.

Forester, C. A. (2001). Body awareness: An aspect of countertransference management that moderates vicarious traumatization. *Dissertation abstracts internationa: Section B: The Sciences and Engineering, 61,* 10-B.

Freud, A. (1937). *Ego and the mechanisms of defense* (rev. ed.). Oxford, UK: Hogarth.

Freud, S. (1922). *Group psychology and the analysis of the ego.* London: International Psychoanalytic Press.

Freud, S. (1953). The future prospects or psychoanalytic therapy. In J. Strachey (Ed. & Trans.), *The standard edition of the complete psychological works of Sigmund Freud* (Vol. 11, pp. 141–151). London: Hogarth Press. (Original work published 1910)

Freud, S. (1953). Observations on transference love. In J. Strachey (Ed. & Trans.), *The standard edition, of the complete psychological works of Sigmund Freud* (Vol. 12, pp. 159–171). London: Hogarth Press. (Original work published 1915)

Gallese, V. (1999). From grasping to language: Mirror neurons and the origin of social communication. In S. Hameroff, A. Kazniak, & D. Chalmers (Eds.), *Towards a science of consciousness* (pp. 165–178). Cambridge, MA: MIT Press.

Gallese, V. (2001). The shared manifold hypothesis. *Journal of Consciousness Studies, 8,* 33–50.

Gallese, V., Fadiga, L., Fogassi, L., & Rizzolatti, G. (1996). Action recognition in the premotor cortex. *Brain,* 119, 593–609.

Gallese, V., Ferrari, P. F., & Umilta, M. A. (2002). The mirror matching system: A shared manifold for intersubjectivity. *Behavioral and Brain Sciences,* 25(1), 35–36.

Gallup, G. G., & Maser, J. D. (1977). Tonic immobility: Evolutionary underpinnings of human catalepsy and catatonia. In M. E. P. Seligman & J. D. Masser (Eds.), *Psychopathology: Experimental models* (pp. 334–357). San Francisco: W.H. Freeman.

Gill, M. M. (1983). The interpersonal paradigm and the degree of the therapist's involvement. *Contemporary Psychoanalysis, 19,* 200–237.

Gill, M. M., & Hoffman, I. Z. (1982). *The analysis of transference,* (Vol. 2). New York: International Universities Press.

Gladstein, G. A. (1984). The historical roots of contemporary empathy research. *Journal of the History of the Behavioral Sciences, 20,* 38–59.

Grandin, T. (2005). *Animals in translation.* New York: Scribner.

Grinberg, L. (1979). Countertransference and projective counteridentification. *Contemporary Psychoanalysis, 15,* 226–247.

Grotstein, J. (1981). *Splitting and projective identification.* Northvale, NJ: Jason Aronson.

Harris, J. C. (2003). Social neuroscience, empathy, brain integration, and neurodevelopmental disorders. *Physiology and Behavior, 79*(3), 525–531.

Hatfield, E., Cacioppo, J. T., & Rapson, R. L. (1992). Emotional contagion. *Review of Personality and Social Psychology, 14,* 151–177.

Hatfield, E., Cacioppo, J. T., & Rapson, R. L. (1994). *Emotional contagion: Studies in emotion and social interaction.* Cambridge, UK: Cambridge University Press.

Hedges, L. (1983). *Listening perspectives in psychotherapy.* Northvale, NJ: Jason Aronson.

Heide, F. J., & Borkovec, T. D. (1983). Relaxation-induced anxiety: Paradoxical anxiety enhancement due to relaxation training. *Journal of Consulting and Clinical Psychology, 51*(2), 171–182.

Hess, U., & Blairy, S. (2001). Facial mimicry and emotional contagion to dynamic emotional facial expressions and their influence on decoding accuracy. *International Journal of Psychophysiology, 40,* 129–141.

Hodges, S. D., & Wegner, D. M. (1997). Automatic and controlled empathy. In W. J. Ickes (Ed.), *Empathic accuracy* (pp. 311–340). New York: Guilford Press.

Hsee, C. K., Hatfield, E., Carlson, J. G., & Chemtob, C. (1990). The effect of power on susceptibility to emotional contagion. *Cognition and Emotion, 4*(4), 327–340.

Jacobsen, E. (1974). *Progressive relaxation: A physiological and clinical investigation of muscular states and their significance in psychology and medical practice* (3rd ed.). Chicago: University of Chicago Press.

James, W. (1884). What is an emotion? *Mind, 9,* 188–205.

Janoff-Bulman, R. (1996). Psychometric review of World Assumption Scale. In B. H. Stamm (Ed.), *Measurement of stress, trauma, and adaptation* (pp. 440–442). Lutherville, MD: Sidran Press.

Kendon, A. (1970). Movement coordination in social interaction: Some examples described. *Acta Psychologica, 32,* 1–25.

Klein, M. (1946). Notes on some schizoid mechanisms. In *The writings of Melanie Klein* (Vol. 3, pp. 1–24). London: Hogarth Press.

Klein, M. (1957). *Envy and gratitude.* New York: Basic Books.

Kohut, H. (1959). Introspection, empathy and psychoanalysis: An examination of the relationship between modes of observation and theory. *Journal of the American Psychoanalytic Association, 7,* 459–483.

Kohut, H. (1971). *The analysis of the self: A systematic approach to the psychoanalytic treatment of narcissistic personality disorders.* New York: International Universities Press.

Kohut, H. (1978). *The search for the self* (Vols. I and II). New York: International Universities Press.

Kohut, H. (1981). *Reflections on empathy.* Lecture tape, University of California, Berkeley extension division, Continuing education seminars, Progress in Self Psychology, Berkeley, California.

LaFrance, M. (1976). Postural sharing as a nonverbal indicator. *Group and Organizational Studies, 1,* 328–333.

LaFrance, M. (1979). Nonverbal synchrony and rapport: Analysis by the cross lag panel technique. *Social Psychology Quarterly, 42,* 66–70.

Lakin, J. L., Jefferis, V. E., Cheng, C. M., & Chartrand, T. L. (2003). The chameleon effect as social glue: Evidence for the evolutionary significance of nonconscious mimicry. *Journal of Nonverbal Behavior, 27*(3), 145–161.

LeDoux, J. E. (1996). *The emotional brain.* New York: Touchstone.

Lehrer, P. M., & Woolfolk, R. L. (1993). Specific effects of stress management techniques. In P. M. Lehrer & R. L. Woolfolk (Eds.), *Principles and practice of stress management* (pp. 481–520). New York: Guilford Press.

Levenson, R. W. (1992). Autonomic nervous system differences among emotions. *Psychological Science, 3*(1), 23–27.

Levenson, R. W., Ekman, P., & Friesen, W. V. (1990). Voluntary facial action generates emotion-specific autonomic nervous system activity. *Psychophysiology, 27*(4), 363–384.

Levenson, R. W., Ekman, P., & Heider, K. (1992). Emotion and autonomic nervous system activity in the Minangkabau of West Sumatra. *Journal of Personality & Social Psychology, 62*(6), 972–988.

Levenson, R. W., & Ruef, A. M. (1997). Physiological aspects of emotional knowledge and rapport. In W. J. Ickes (Ed.), *Empathic accuracy* (pp. 44–72). New York: Guilford Press.

Lipps, T. (1964). Archiv für die gestamte. In M. Rader (Ed.), *A modern book of esthetics: An anthology* (3rd ed.). New York: Holt, Rinehart, and Winston. (Reprinted from *Psychologie, 1,* 1903)

Little, M. (1957). "R"—The analyst's response to his patient's needs. *International Journal of Psycho-Analysis, 60,* 357–373.

MacDougall, W. (1908). *An introduction to social psychology.* Boston: Luce.

MacLean, P. D. (1973). *A triune concept of the brain and behaviour: Hincks memorial lecture.* Oxford: University of Toronto Press.

Maslach, C., & Jackson, S. E. (1986). *Maslach Burnout Inventory: Human services survey.* Palo Alto, CA: CPP.

Maxfield, L. (1997). *Advanced clinical interventions: A training manual for work with survivors of trauma, abuse, and violence.* Thunder Bay, ON Author.

McCann, L., & Pearlman, L. A. (1990). Vicarious traumatization: A framework for understanding the psychological effects of working with victims. *Journal of Traumatic Stress, 3,* 131–149.

McClintock, M. K. (1971). Menstrual synchrony and suppression. *Nature, 229,* 244–245.

Meltzoff, A. N., & Moore, M. K. (1983). Newborn infants imitate adult facial gestures. *Child Development, 54,* 702–709.

Meltzoff, A. N., & Moore, M. K. (1989). Imitation in newborn infants: Exploring the range of gestures imitated and the underlying mechanisms. *Developmental Psychology, 25,* 954–962.

Merriam-Webster's collegiate dictionary (10th ed.). (1996). Springfield, MA:

Merriam-Webster.

Miller, K. I., Stiff, J. B., & Ellis, B. H. (1988). Communication and empathy as precursors to burnout among human service workers. *Communication Monographs, 55*(3), 250–265.

Morris, D. (1979). *Manwatching: A field guide to human behavior.* New York: Henry N. Abrahams.

Nadel, L., & Jacobs, W. J. (1996). The role of the hippocampus in PTSD, panic, and phobia. In N. Kato (Ed.), *Hippocampus: Functions and clinical relevance* (pp. 455–463). Amsterdam: Elsevier.

Napier, N. (1996). *Recreating your self: Increasing self-esteem through imaging and self-hypnosis.* New York: Norton.

Niedenthal, P. M., Barsalou, L., Winkielman, P., Krauth-Gruber, S., & Ric, F. (in press). Embodiment in attitudes, social perception, and emotion. *Personality and Social Psychology Review.*

Paccalin, C., & Jeannerod, M. (2000). Changes in breathing during observation of effortful actions. *Brain Research, 862,* 194–200.

Parsons, L. M., Fox, P. T., Downs, J. H., Glass, T., Hirsch, T. B., Martin, C. C., et al. (1995). Use of implicit motor imagery for visual shape discrimination as revealed by PET. *Nature, 375,* 54–58.

Pearlman, L. A., & Saakvitne, K. W. (1995). *Trauma and the therapist: Countertransference and vicarious traumatization in psychotherapy with incest survivors.* New York: Norton.

Pines, A., & Maslach, C. (1978). Characteristics of staff burnout in mental health settings. *Hospital and Community Psychiatry, 29*(4), 233–237.

Platek, S. M., Critton, S. R., Meyers, T. E. (2003). Contagious yawning: the role of self-awareness and mental state attribution. *Cognitive Brain Research, 17*(2), 223–227.

Poe, E. A. (1984). The purloined letter. In *Complete stories and poems of Edgar Allan Poe.* New York: Doubleday.

Porges, S. (1995). Orienting in a defensive world: Mammalian modifications of our evolutionary heritage. A Polyvagal Theory. *Psychophysiology, 32,* 301–318.

Porges, S. (2003). The Polyvagal Theory: Phylogenetic contributions to social behavior. *Physiology & Behavior, 79,* 503–513.

Preston, S. D., & de Waal, F. B. M. (2002). Empathy: Its ultimate and proximate bases. *Behavioral and Brain Sciences, 25*(1), 1–72.

Ramachandran, V. S. (2000). Mirror neurons and imitation learning as the driving force behind "the great leap forward" in human evolution. *Edge 69.* Retrieved August 1, 2005, from http://www.edge.org/documents/archive/edge69.html.

Reich, W. (1972). *Character analysis.* New York: Touchstone.

Reik, T. (1948). *Listening with the third ear.* New York: Grove Press.

Restak, R. (1995). *Brainscapes: An introduction to what neuroscience has learned about the structure, function, and abilities of the brain.* New York: Hyperion.

Rizzolatti, G., & Arbib, M. A. (1998). Language within my grasp. *Trends in Neuroscience, 21,* 188–194.

Rizzolatti, G., Fadiga, L., Gallese, V., & Fogassi, L. (1996). Premotor cortex and the recognition of motor actions. *Cognitive Brain Research, 3*(2), 131–141.

Rogers, C. R. (1946). Significant aspects of client centered therapy. *American Psychologist, 1,* 415–422.

Rogers, C. R. (1951). *Client centered therapy.* Boston: Houghton-Mifflin.

Rosenheck, R., & Nathan, P. (1985). Secondary traumatization in children of Vietnam veterans. *Hospital and Community Psychiatry, 36*(5), 538–539.

Rothschild, B. (2000). *The body remembers: The psychophysiology of trauma and trauma treatment.* New York: Norton.

Rothschild, B. (2002a). Case studies: The dangers of empathy. *Psychotherapy Networker, 16,* 4.

Rothschild, B. (2002b). The mind and body of vicarious traumatization: Help for the therapist. *Psychotherapy in Australia, 8,* 2.

Rothschild, B. (2003). *The body remembers casebook: Unifying methods and models in the treatment of trauma and PTSD.* New York: Norton.

Rothschild, B. (2004a). Applying the brakes. *Psychotherapy Networker, 28*(1), 42–45, 66.

Rothschild, B. (2004b). Mirror, mirror. *Psychotherapy Networker, 28*(5), 46–50, 69.

Rothschild, B., & Shiffrar, M. (2003b, 2004). [Postural mirroring and somatic empathy]. Unpublished raw data.

Rothschild, B., & Shiffrar, M. (2004). *Pilot Help for the Helper training course.* Unpublished raw data.

Rothschild, B., Shiffrar, M., & Turner, E. J. (2005). *Applications of mirroring and unmirroring in a practice setting.* Unpublished raw data.

Scheler, M. (1912). *The nature of sympathy.* Hamden, CT: Archon Books, 1972.

Schoenewolf, G. (1990). Emotional contagion: Behavioral induction in individuals and group. *Modern Psychoanalysis, 15*(1), 49–61.

Schore, A. (1994). *Affect regulation and the origin of the self.* Hillsdale, NJ: Lawrence Erlbaum Associates.

Schore, A. (2002) Clinical implications of a psychoneurobiological model of projective identification. In S. Alhanati (Ed.), *Primitive mental states: Psychobiological and psychoanalytic perspectives on early trauma and personality development* (pp. 1–65). Los Angeles: Other Press.

Schore, A. (2003). *Affect regulation and the repair of the self.* New York: Norton.

Shalev, A. Y., Peri, T., Canetti, L., & Schreiber, S. (1996). Predictors of PTSD in injured trauma survivors: A prospective study. *American Journal of Psychiatry, 153*(2), 219–225.

Shindul-Rothschild, J. (2001). Terrorism and Trauma: Psychiatric Nursing Implications. Slide show prepared as a presentation for the Rhode Island State Nurses Association. Retrieved October 2, 2004 from http://www.

risnarn.org/presentations/2001_pstd/.

Siegel, E. V. (1984). *Dance-movement therapy: Mirror of my selves; the psychoanalytic approach*. New York: Human Sciences Press.

Solomon, M. F. (1989). *Narcissim and intimacy*. New York: Norton.

Solomon, Z., Waysman, M., & Levy, G. (1992). From front line to home front: A study of secondary traumatization. *Family Process, 31*(3), 289–302.

Stamm, B. H. (1995). *Secondary traumatic stress: Self-care issues for clinicians, researchers, and educators*. Baltimore: Sidran Press.

Stamm, B. H. (1996). *Measurement of stress, trauma, and adaptation*. Lutherville, MD: Sidran Press.

Stanek, B., Hahn, R., & Mayer, H. (1973). Biometric findings on cardiac neurosis. III. Changes in ECG and heart rate in cardiophobic patients and their doctor during psychoanalytical initial interviews. *Psychotherapy and Psychosomatics, 22*, 289–299.

Stark, M. (1999). *Modes of therapeutic action: Enhancement of knowledge, provision of experience, and engagement in relationship*. Northvale, NJ: Jason Aronson.

Stern, D. N. (1992). Commentary on constructivism in clinical psychoanalysis. *Psychoanalytic Dialogues, 2*, 331–363.

Stern, D. N. (Speaker). (2002). Conference: *Attachment: From early childhood through the lifespan* (Cassette Recording No. 609–617). Los Angeles: Lifespan Learning Institute.

Stiff, J. B., Dillard, J. P., & Somera, L. (1988). Empathy, communication, and prosocial behavior. *Communication Monographs, 55*(2), 198–213.

Stolorow, R., & Atwood, G. (1992). *Contexts of being: The intersubjective foundations of psychological life*. Hillsdale, NJ: Analytic Press.

Stolorow, R., Atwood, G., & Orange, D. (2002). Worlds of experience: Interweaving philosophical and clinical dimensions in psychoanalysis. New York: Basic Books

Strack, F., Martin, L., & Strepper, W. (1988). Inhibiting and facilitating conditions of the human smile: A nonobtrusive test of the facial feedback hypothesis. *Journal of Personality and Social Psychology, 54*(5), 768–777.

Sullivan, H. S. (1947). *Conceptions of modern psychiatry*. Washington, DC: White Foundation.

Sullivan, H. S. (1954). *The psychiatric interview*. New York: Norton.

Tauber, Y. (1998). *In the other chair*. Jerusalem: Gefen.

Terr, L. C. (1985). Psychic trauma in children and adolescents. *Psychiatric Clinics of North America, 8*(4), 815–835.

Titchener, E. B. (1909). *Lectures on the experimental psychology of the thought processes*. New York: Macmillan.

Tompkins, S. S. (1963). *Affect, imagery, consciousness* (2 Vols.). New York: Springer.

van der Kolk, B. A. (1996). The complexity of adaptation to trauma: self-regulation, stimulus discrimination, and characteriological development. In B. A. van der Kolk, A. C. McFarlane, & L. Weisaeth (Eds.), *Traumatic Stress* (pp. 182–213). New York: Guilford Press.

van der Kolk, B. A., McFarlane, A. C., & Weisaeth, L. (Eds.). (1996). *Traumatic stress*. New York: Guilford Press.

Waysman, M., Mikulincer, M., & Solomon, Z. (1993). Secondary traumatization among wives of posttraumatic combat veterans: A family typology. *Journal of Family Psychology, 7*(1), 104–118.

Weller, L., & Weller, A. (1993). Human menstrual synchrony. *Neuroscience and Biobehavioral Reviews, 17*(4), 427–439.

Whipple, D. (1986). Discussion of the merits and problems with "The concept of projective identification" by Janet Finell. *Psychoanalytic Review, 73*(2), 121–128.

Wilson, J. P., & Lindy, J. D. (Eds.). (1994). *Countertransference in the treatment of PTSD*. New York: Guilford Press.

Wolf, N. S., Gales, M., Shane, E. (2000). Mirror neurons, procedural learning, and the positive new experience: A developmental systems self psychology approach. *Journal of the American Academy of Psychoanalysis & Dynamic Psychiatry, 28*(3), 409–430.

Wolf, N. S., Gales, M. E., Shane, E., & Shane, M. (2001). The developmental trajectory from amodal perception to empathy and communication: The role of mirror neurons in this process. *Psychoanalytic Inquiry, 21*(1), 94–112.

Wolpe, J. (1969). *The practice of behavior therapy*. London: Pergamon Press.

Zajonc, R. B., Adelmann, P. K., Murphy, S. T., & Niedenthal, P. M. (1987). Convergence in the physical appearance of spouses. *Motivation and Emotion, 11*(4), 335–346.

Index